wings

A MEMOIR

BIRDS WITHOUT wings

A MEMOIR

REINA MURRAY *with*
SYLVESTER I. OKORO

TATE PUBLISHING & *Enterprises*

Published by Tate Publishing & Enterprises, LLC
127 E. Trade Center Terrace | Mustang, Oklahoma 73064 USA
1.888.361.9473 | www.tatepublishing.com

Tate Publishing is committed to excellence in the publishing industry. The company reflects the philosophy established by the founders, based on Psalms 68:11,
"The Lord gave the word and great was the company of those who published it."

Book design copyright © 2007 by Tate Publishing, LLC. All rights reserved.
Cover design by Liz Mason
Interior design by Sarah Leis

Published in the United States of America
Library of Congress Cataloging-in-publication data
Murray, Reina
Birds Without Wings: A book of hope, victory and freedom / Reina Murray with Sylvester
I. Okoro

ISBN:978-1-6024700-1-9
07.06.19

THE HOLY SPIRIT

You were there!
Seconds before I was conceived, you were there,
As I fought my way through the birth canal
And was thrust into this world.
I lay still, lifeless, eyes shut, and no movement.
You formed yourself into breath and filled my
lungs.
My life began...because you were there.
I screamed violently,
Not understanding even the comfort of a mother's
embrace.
You formed yourself into a shield of love in my
mother's arms,
And I felt love for the first time...because you
were there.
In my youth, still without full knowledge of you,
Thinking you were an it, a thing,
I used you at will.
When my friends were around, I concealed you.
When they broke my heart, I cried a thousand tears
in your bosom.
You formed yourself into a blanket of comfort,
And I found peace...because you were there.
Young adulthood brought with it insecurities,
Lack of direction,
A sense of loneliness.

You formed yourself into a rope,
Wrapping yourself around me gently,
Guiding me through the most difficult time in my life.
I found security... because you were there.
With maturity came lost dreams,
Puzzled visions,
Knowledge without wisdom.
I proclaimed you without knowing you.
Feeling you without touching you.
Loving you without being in love with you.
Straddling the fence,
Drifting out to sea,
Seeing the shore without touching it.
You formed yourself into a piece of driftwood,
Floating me back to shore.
Teaching me, guiding me, loving me,
You became my friend.
And finally I realized...
you were there all the time!

Acknowledgments

To my husband, Larry Murray, who has taught me a love that makes forgiving possible. Larry, I *am* because *we* are. You give "soulmate" a new meaning. Thank you for decades of unconditional love and support. Thanks for allowing me the space and the time to tap into the uncharted waters of becoming a writer. I love you now and forever.

To my five children, you are birds *with* wings! It makes me proud to see how high each one of you has soared, only because you believed you could fly.

To my grandchildren, you have given me the greatest gift any woman could ask for—the gift of being a nana. I love you more than you know. My wish for you is love and happiness always.

To my God children, thank you!

To Sylvester I. Okoro, MBA, thank you for being the kind of person about whom one can write something good and not feel hard-pressed. You got into the trenches, kept me on track, encouraged me when I doubted myself, helped me find my writer's voice, and made me use it. Although *Birds Without Wings* is my story, without you, the book might have remained merely a passing idea. Therefore, *Birds Without Wings* is *our* book. You have been more than a co-author. You have been a mentor, coach, partner, role model, leader, and collaborator. In fact, I have grown because of your generosity. I will always be indebted to you. You are an editor's editor.

To Paul Weisser, Ph.D., you have encouraged me as a writer to connect more directly and personally with my readers. Your suggestions and criticisms were clear, and wise. Throughout the process, you have maintained a great sense of humor, and in my submission, every writer needs a Paul Weisser.

To my siblings, I love you!

To my spiritual sisterhood—Rhonda, Dwanna, Dion, and Max-amillion—I thank you for teaching me that often the way out is the way back, and that sometimes the road to your future leads through your past. Your message has been heard loud and clear: letting go of the painful past will help you experience the joy of the present. Thanks for pushing and pulling me through this journey called writing.

Finally, to my reader, Sharon Flood, and all my adopted children from Vizions, and my photographer, Cameron L. Duncan, thank you!

REINA MURRAY

1

Disbelief

Anticipating the journey did not allow me to get a decent night's sleep. I was physically prepared for the trip—my bags were packed, waiting at the door—but emotionally I was a wreck, drifting back and forth from past to present. My past had held me in bondage. For the last few days, I had been on an emotional roller coaster, which would prove to be as scary as the first time I had ever ridden on a real roller coaster.

I was sixteen—a naïve country girl who had never even been to an amusement park or seen cotton candy before. But nevertheless, my life had been exceptional. Dad had agreed to let me spend the summer in DC with my oldest sister, Joyce. That was the first time I was away from my father and stepmother for any length of time. Dad was catering to my every whim, since I had just experienced a devastating loss.

For a brief moment, I forgot about the past, hypnotized by the lights, the smell of popcorn, and all the people laughing and having fun around me. This was just the distraction I needed.

As I climbed onto the roller coaster, I wondered why everyone was screaming. I didn't want anyone with me in the car. I could tackle this demon alone. The ride operator was a young man my own age. As he checked my seat belt, he looked into my eyes, and I looked away. He reminded me of Marshall, and that was the last thing I wanted to be thinking about.

While the car began the long slow pull up the hill, my excitement began to mount. The heat of the sun shining on my face was so warm and inviting that I lay my head back, relaxed, enjoying the moment of solitude.

What a piece of cake! I thought.

But just then my body jerked back. I quickly looked up and realized I was in a free-fall, twisting and turning in a circular motion. I clung to the bar in front of me until my fingers ached. My stomach began to turn in knots. With perspiration beading over my forehead, I started vomiting without control, and tears began running down my face. I thought I was going to die.

Please, God, don't let me die!

And then, as quickly as the ride began, it came to an abrupt stop. How foolish I must have looked to all the people climbing out of their seats. But I was only a country girl who would never willingly give up control of her life again. At that very moment, I began to conceal my past. I would simply never discuss it with anyone, as if it never took place.

My memory of that roller coaster ride, which was both my first and my last, was interrupted by my oldest daughter as she walked into the room. Picking up one of my bags, she urged me to hurry. I started giving her final orders, possibly for the tenth time, about how to run the house while I was gone. She was so much like her dad, how could I not love her? Our bond was closer than just mother and daughter. I had made a solemn vow to God long before she was born to love her unconditionally. That wasn't hard, because she was so hungry for love. She was from my husband's prior marriage, but she was still mine because the word *step* was never allowed in our family. All the children belonged to us. They were gifts from God, regardless of who gave birth to them.

It was my middle daughter who was my challenge. She loved me, but she also felt that her love was a betrayal of her biological mother. Ironically, she looked more like me than she did her mother. I just wanted her to know that she could have two mothers and love both of them without feeling guilty. I had promised to give unconditional love to all my children—even before they were born.

I had made that promise when I was only eleven, right after I met my stepmother.

The first time I met Mamie, I was amazed at how big she was—five feet eleven, with legs shaped like baseball bats, and huge hands. Her eyes were small, with black rings around them from using bleaching cream to lighten her complexion. She had a wide mouth full of gold dentures, which she would often pop out when she wasn't sucking on them, making a horrible clicking sound.

I was the youngest of her four stepchildren. Since I had just arrived from Boston, I didn't quite understand the household rules. My sisters and brother kept warning me that this day would come, but still I didn't know what would happen, so I wasn't prepared.

My dad, who was in the Coast Guard, had left the night before. He was so handsome in his white military uniform. I was sad that he was leaving, because I had only been living with him for a week. He assured me that his three months at sea would go fast, but his eyes didn't look very reassuring.

As I rushed home from school, I realized that this was the first day that my dad would not be home, or at least on his way home from work. When I entered the house through the back of the garage, as Mamie insisted all her stepchildren do, I performed the usual rituals and ran into the house to see my siblings. Mamie immediately ordered me to go to my brother's room.

The moment I stepped through the door, I was stricken with horror. What I saw reminded me of what my siblings had warned me about. It was all true.

Mamie shrieked at my sister Joyce, "Strip off all your clothes!"

I felt that I had just stepped onto a horror movie set. I couldn't hear a thing Mamie was saying, because of the deafening screams in my head. As I stood there, looking at my brother, Walter, who was just entering puberty, tears began to well up in my eyes. I had never seen a man's genitals before. I stared at him in disbelief. He looked away ashamed.

Everything moved in slow motion. Mamie gestured toward the

bed. Joyce, who was completely naked by now, walked over to the bed with her head up and lay face down, holding the bedpost. She turned to look at me with as much reassurance as she could. Lying there, a fully developed woman, she showed no shame in front of her brother, who refused to look at her body.

Suddenly, the screams in my head got louder. Looking up, I realized they were coming from my sister as an electrical cord was slung wantonly at her body. Welts formed on her skin as her body jerked with each blow. Sheer panic began to envelop me. The space somehow got smaller, and my body began to shake.

Oh, my God! Let me live through this nightmare, and I swear I will never treat a child this way in my life. I swear!

My son's voice interrupted my recollection of the past as he walked into the room.

"Mom, where are you? We've been calling you for the last five minutes."

I quickly turned away to hide the tears in my eyes. My past was so painful. The moment I decided to face Mamie for the first time in over twenty years, the memories I had suppressed so successfully up till now started flooding my thoughts.

Today, Mamie couldn't have gotten away with all the abuse she inflicted on us. Since then, many laws have been passed against child abuse, and people are speaking up against it. In the sixties and early seventies, however, children were at the mercy of their parents or guardians. It saddens me to think that some children were silenced forever. We were raised in the South in the era of who "spareth his rod hateth his son" (Proverbs 13:24). Consequently, the authorities actually believed that corporal punishment was essential for bringing up a child.

"Mom, did you hear me calling you?"

"I'm coming," I said, wiping away the tears.

As I looked up into my son's face, I could see the strength I had instilled in him for the past fifteen years. I had willed every part of my being to him, praying that he would be a strong, independent, and stable man. But at this moment, I could see that he was very worried about my journey.

Over the years, I had told my children that I had endured a painful childhood, but I had never gone into the excruciating details about it, too ashamed to reveal the total humiliation we had suffered from our stepmother. Somehow my past secrets had now turned on me.

My son had always been able to read me and feel my pain. I felt as if his spirit had been there with me when I was a child, helping me to survive those bitter years. Now he was willing me back the strength I had bestowed on him. Wrapping his arms around me, he jokingly said, "It's okay, Mom...you're my *she*-ro."

The ride to the airport was filled with teary eyes, nervous smiles, jittery touches, and lots of broken glances. We all hugged at the airport gate. Then, as I kissed my youngest daughter, she began pleading to go with me. I smiled, knowing full well that she would never get on the plane. At seven, her fear of flying was much greater than her fear of me leaving.

This was the first time I had ever left my family, and they were not taking it lightly. As I looked into my young daughter's eyes, I could see her profound sadness. She was my miracle child—the one I was never supposed to have. Again, I was swept away into my past.

Mamie was always chanting: "If you ever let a man touch you inappropriately, you'll get pregnant. And when you have a baby, every bone in your body will open. And if the bones don't close properly, you'll be crippled forever!"

Needless to say, this image was etched in my mind. After I had six miscarriages, my doctors finally realized that I had a severe problem, since they could find no physical reasons for the miscarriages. As much as I wanted to give birth, my fear of having a child was apparently greater than my desire to have one. I had nightmares of dying during labor. Finally, I realized that my mind was playing tricks on me, which meant that Mamie was winning over me psychologically. At that point, I decided to seek therapeutic help.

Through therapy and relaxation techniques, I was eventually able to carry my son to full term. I was pregnant eight times and only gave birth twice. The doctors informed me after my son was born that I only had one tube, and it was nonfunctional.

Ten years after my son was born, and with no indication beforehand, I found myself pregnant with what turned out to be my youngest daughter. Every day I had to remind myself that childbirth was natural, and that I wouldn't be crippled for life. I had to fight for the life that was growing inside me, believing she was a miracle, and I couldn't let my mind abort this miracle that God had created. He had given me another chance, and I had to pass the test.

As I boarded the plane, I turned to look back at my family. It was so painful leaving them. Or was it facing my past that was painful? I was certain my husband could handle things while I was away. A smile came over my face as I looked at him standing there, being so strong for the children. The whole burden was now on his shoulders. And what capable shoulders they were!

Larry was the total opposite of my father in some ways, and then there were similarities between them that were uncanny. He was a warm and sensitive man, not afraid of bathing the kids or cooking the meals. Even changing diapers was just another part of parenting to him. His strength is what I admired most about him. It was a gentle strength, not overbearing or possessive, a confident reassuring strength that comes from one's life experiences. He came from a very large family, with eleven brothers and sisters and two parents. He was very protective of his family. I would joke and call him "my knight." If only my father had been strong, how different our lives could have been.

My grandmother had abandoned my father when he was only five years old, and left him to be raised by one of her sisters, who had no children. Aunt Minnie's love for him was endless, but it could never fill the void in his soul that abandonment had left behind.

Giving us all the love he could, this gentle, sensitive man was as weak as he was loving. He had suffered terribly, wondering why his mother had left him. He was ripped from his sisters and brothers and given away like a possession, and this had made him totally vulnerable. Sometimes, our greatest fears are the ones that haunt us and cause us to make decisions in our lives that will forever affect the way we live. His only dream was that his own children have at least one parent raise them for better or for worse. And for worse it was.

"Hello," a voice rang out from in front of me, and I realized again that I had drifted back to the past. It was the pilot, greeting me as I boarded the plane.

This would be a four-hour flight. Questions began to flood my thoughts. *What will I say to them? How will they look? Will I be able to vent my anger?*

For twenty years, I had dreamed of facing my oppressor, expressing the anger and hatred that I had carried inside for so long. Suddenly, the motion of the plane gaining altitude began to turn my stomach. *Oh, I know just what to do.*

This routine was so familiar to me. I would relax, close my eyes, and take slow deep breaths.

Once the plane reached its peak altitude, I switched off the overhead light, pulled down the window shade, and lay back in my seat. My palms were sweaty, and beads of moisture trickled down my neck and forehead. Breathing deeply, I began to compose myself.

I made it without throwing up, unlike many other times when I had been stressed. My life was filled with tears and nausea. As I calmed down, my mind wandered off to the first time I could recall getting nauseous.

2

Academy of Terror

It was right after the horrible scene I had walked in on with my brother and sisters. Actually, I can only recall bits and pieces of my childhood before that.

Every night, as I lay in bed, I was afraid to close my eyes. Because the moment I did, the room would slowly begin to spin around—very slowly at first, and then my bed would begin to twirl. As it began to move, my body would be whirling through a tunnel, and the nightmares would start.

In one of them, there was a little white rabbit, who seemed so gentle and harmless. But the closer I got, the bigger he became, until he was a giant with huge teeth. Then he would begin to chase me through a tunnel, trying to devour me. As I reached the end of the tunnel, he would always jump out in front of me. Usually, I would wake up at that moment, terrifying everyone in the house with my horrifying screams. I lived in a nightmare by day and was haunted with nightmares by night.

My sister Joyce, who was fifteen, was the oldest of the four of us, and tried to comfort us the best she could. She was so old for her age. Joyce was the woman of the house in every way other than sexual. She also didn't get to issue out any discipline. That was Mamie's job. Joyce tried to be the voice of reason, always rationalizing and smoothing things over to avoid our getting a beating. Her daily routine was to make everything in the house run smoothly, and she was as close to perfect as one could get.

Joyce had soft shoulder-length dark hair, which framed her

small face. Her complexion was soft milky chocolate, which I often admired. She was only a little over five feet tall, and was quite gentle... until she was provoked. Then her small frame would somehow seem to double in size. On the rare occasion when she did get angry, we all knew to back down. Joyce always held her head up high, as if she were the tallest among us. She was our role model. The more Mamie tried to tear her down emotionally and physically, the more Joyce looked like she had just won a marathon race. Actually, this was her silent independent protest of Mamie's inhumane treatment. Joyce didn't know how beautiful she was.

She was the spitting image of Mother. That's what we always had to call our real mother. We were never allowed to call her Mama. The fact that Joyce looked so much like Mother was a threat to Mamie, who punished her with verbal bashings. Joyce was never allowed to look too nice. Many times, Mamie sent her back to her room to change her clothes, and also forced her to wear outdated thick glasses.

At 5:30 a.m. in the morning, Joyce was the first to wake up. The winters were extremely difficult for us. Although we were in the heart of the South, the temperatures were often below zero. Each morning, Joyce would put her coat over the top of her sleepwear, go out to the garage, take off her house slippers, step into her outside shoes, run to the clothesline, and get our wash rags. Returning to the garage, she would step out of her shoes, line them up perfectly with the others, and slide her house slippers back on. Only then could she reenter the house. After washing up and preparing herself for the day, she would wake up the rest of us.

Each of us had five minutes in the bathroom and ten minutes to get dressed. At exactly 6:00 a.m., we were in the garage eating our breakfast at a table placed in the corner. It literally took us only a few seconds to gulp down our breakfast, which usually consisted of soggy cornflakes without sugar and two tablespoons of canned milk mixed with water.

If we were lucky, Joyce would let us sneak in sugar. But she was very careful, because if she allowed something forbidden and we were caught, all of us would get the same punishment.

By 6:15 a.m., our chores began. Joyce had to clean the kitchen and dust-mop all the floors. We had hardwood floors throughout the house, which glowed in the dark.

Joyce's strength was one of her greatest qualities. On many occasions, she would swallow her pride and cater to Mamie, hoping to penetrate her hard shell. On the few occasions that it worked, she would simply say, "Believe in the unexpected!" She was wise beyond her years.

Pat was the next oldest. She was only a year younger than Joyce, but they were as opposite as night and day. Pat's frame was larger than Joyce's from the age of three on. Even at fourteen, Pat had the shape of a twenty-year-old beauty. She had long shapely legs and curves in all the right places. Her thick black hair was often pulled back into a ponytail. She had high cheek bones and eyes you could get lost in. Her lips were full and shapely. Her complexion was dark brown. She was the darkest among us, and Mamie would often try to use her color as a weapon, calling her either "blackie" or "darkie."

Pat's facial expressions often revealed her anger. She had a small thin nose, like Mother's, and when she was angry, her nostrils would flare up. As a result, she was often caught rolling her eyes or smacking her lips. Pat found it very difficult to cover her anger.

Pat's daily chores were to polish every piece of furniture in the house. She was supplied with two rags, one to apply the polish, the other to wipe it down afterward. There was no way for her to cut corners. She had to move everything off each piece of furniture and put it back only after the furniture was dusted and waxed. Then every object had to be put back *exactly* where it had been. Needless to say, Pat tested Mamie's ability to remember things, and always got a kick out of trying to make her look stupid by moving things around. Pat's anger was easy for Mamie to see through, so Mamie often beat or tormented Pat simply so she could demonstrate she was in control.

One incident remains engraved in my mind. The house was freezing, and we were running behind schedule because no one wanted to get out of bed. Joyce sent Pat to the clothesline to get the rags for our morning wash-up. Pat started mumbling how pathetic it was that the linen closet was filled with brand new washcloths, and we had never been allowed to use any of them. Instead, Mamie had ordered Joyce to take an old towel and tear it into pieces. Each of us got a piece, and that's what we used for our washcloth as long as I can remember.

On that particular freezing morning, Pat woke up angry and was in rare form. She began throwing things around and yelling. She was furious that we were never allowed to leave those pathetic scraps of rags in the immaculate bathroom. The moment the last person washed, whoever had towel duty had to go outside to the clothesline and hang out the rags. It goes without saying that our bath towels were ratty old strings no longer capable of absorbing water.

Pat was mumbling about the conditions of the towels as she snatched them up to take them outside.

From out of nowhere, Mamie appeared. Lashing out, she began striking Pat across the back of her head and along the side of her face.

"Keep your mouth shut!" she screamed.

Pat was startled. As she turned around to face Mamie, her body stiffened and her jaws tightened. She stood glaring at Mamie as the big woman walked away. Pat grunted defiantly. She didn't say a word, just grunted like a caged animal wanting to strike out, but knowing that invisible bars restricted her.

Mamie quickly turned back and struck her across the face a second time. Pat grunted again and her body reared up. This exchange went on for about five minutes. With each blow to Pat's face, a new bruise formed. Her full lips began to swell.

I was standing there, not daring to speak out. My eyes were begging Pat to stop. *Please stop! You can't win!*

Finally, Mamie left, but quickly returned with the electrical cord. "Go to your room," she yelled at Pat. "And strip!"

Pat went into her room and slowly began to take off her clothes. She was pacing back and forth like a caged panther, staring at Mamie without ever looking away. She reached behind her back to unzip her dress, let it drop to the floor, and stepped away from it, still glaring and pacing. Then she unfastened her bra and slung it against the wall. Finally, she slowly slipped her panties down, allowing them to slide off her body.

Hatred engulfed the room as she walked over to the bed, stretching her body out over the blankets while holding on to the iron post that framed the head of the bed. Her glare never changed, never broke.

The cord began to cut into her flesh over and over again, but her stare was unyielding. Not a sound escaped from her lips, even though her body twitched with each blow as her flesh yielded to the punishment. The lashes became more savage. As more and more welts formed on her skin, her stare finally broke, and tears began to fall. She cried out like a wild animal. Broken, she had lost this battle, but her private war was still going on inside.

Witnessing this from the hallway, my body went limp. I slid down the wall and began to shed tears.

Walter, who was thirteen when I arrived, was the third child, and my father's only son. He took the place that Dad should have had as our protector. Walter was shorter than other boys of his age, and resembled Dad. His hair was always cut short, and his body was already quite masculine. He had large hands, and his complexion was almost the same milky chocolate as Joyce's. Walter had deep-set eyes and incredibly long eyelashes. He rarely laughed, but when he did, he had a smile that was contagious. He often looked sad, gloomy, remorseful, and even defeated. Being my father's only biological male child, he felt compelled to take action when Mamie went on her rampages. Often he would take the blame for us, and suffer the punishment. But there were many times that he couldn't protect us, and then he felt terribly guilty.

Walter's daily chores consisted of emptying the trash can, cleaning the garage, maintaining the lawn, and performing the "shoe detail," which was another of Mamie's perverted obsessions. Walter had to take a bucket of hot soapy water twice a day and wash off the soles of all the shoes in the garage. At the end of the day, he had to bring the shoes inside the house, one pair for each of us, and place them in our closets. This was pretty freakish, given that we were never allowed to wear shoes in the house anyway. Nevertheless, it was one of Walter's daily humiliations.

If Mamie were not around, we would slip off our shoes and wash off the bottoms ourselves. Then we would leave them at the outside entrance to the house and tell Walter they were already done.

Although Walter was a bright student, school was very hard for him because of his often uncontrollable temper. He always got into fights. In fact, he didn't just fight, he tried to stomp the life out of any student brave enough to confront him. The teachers were confused by him because his work was always prepared, and understanding schoolwork was natural for him. Walter was my father's brightest child, but his rage was always just below the surface.

Walter became a "runner." That is, he ran away any time life became unbearable for him and he felt he could no longer protect us. The school administrators would allow him to come back because he was the top athlete in the school. For his entire four years in high school, he excelled in all sports. But in order for him to play, he sometimes had to run away from home.

There was one occasion when Mamie decided to be vengeful because Walter hadn't arrived home on time. He was ten minutes late because football practice had run a little over. When he came running into the house, he explained this to Mamie. She didn't say a single word until the next day when he was preparing for the game. Then she announced that he would not be able to play or even attend the game. Walter was devastated that he wouldn't be able to participate in the homecoming game.

We all felt terrible for him because he had worked so hard for the starting position on the football team, and our disappointment threw the entire house into a state of depression.

That evening, when Mamie retired early to her bedroom, Walter simply dressed for the game, packed some clothes, and announced to us that he was leaving.

I couldn't believe he was actually going to disobey her and leave, but he did.

During the game, he scored the winning touchdown, which won

the game for his team. So he was a celebrity at school but a runaway at home.

I was a perfect mix of Mother and Dad. Mother was fair-skinned, and Dad was dark. I had Daddy's big brown eyes and Mother's full and perfectly shaped lips. My hair, which I usually wore in two ponytails, was thick and long, and the curls were so tight that my hair was hard to control. At eleven, I was very thin, and my teeth were too big for my mouth. I was timid and afraid. My stepfather had already secretly introduced me to fear.

My chores were to clean the blinds in the house every day and to wipe off the window sills. I was supplied with a bucket of water, a wet towel, and a second towel for drying. The task wasn't as simple as just dusting the blinds. Each blade had to be wiped individually. So each morning, I went throughout the house and did all twenty-five blinds. If Mamie touched one blade and found a speck of dust on it, she would beat me when I came home from school.

Most of my school day was spent worrying about what she would find out of place and which one of us she would unleash her anger against when we arrived home. Often she beat one of us a day, and sometimes her vengeance was so brutal that she would beat all of us. She didn't quite abuse me as much as the rest. I don't know if it was because I was the youngest or because my siblings constantly tried to protect me. Or maybe it was because I was my father's baby. "Reesa" is what they called me, and Dad always called me "Reesa Baby."

Sometimes, something as simple as not folding our underwear perfectly, or leaving a wrinkle in our bed, or even hanging a garment in the closet in the wrong direction warranted severe punishment.

I tried to stay away from Mamie as much as possible. I cried so much that she thought I was pathetic and often didn't want to have anything to do with a "crybaby."

On the other hand, I would cheer up Joyce, Pat, and Walter by telling them stories about my life with our mother and our younger siblings. They never got to know grandmother and hear about all of life's remedies from her, but they did get to know her and her wisdom through me. I had so much of my mother in me because she had raised me for the first eleven years of my life. The others would cling to the stories I would tell them about her, as if I were giving them a part of her.

At night, I would often lie in bed and read. We were not allowed to keep the lights on after we went to bed, so I usually only had the light of the moon to read by. These were my quiet stolen moments. Helen Keller and Heidi were my favorite characters. I would read about them over and over again, losing myself in the stories of their miracles. It freed me to know that God had a reason for everything. I was expecting my own miracle any day. I didn't realize then that it was God's way of increasing my faith. He had smiled on me and given me invincible faith that would carry me through life.

And then there was "Stolen Boy." That's what we called him when Mamie wasn't around. My siblings had told me about him, but he was not a reality until I was actually face to face with him.

About five years earlier, Mamie's best friend had had an extra-marital affair while her husband was off in the military, and had conceived a child. The day she left the hospital, Mamie brought the boy home as her own. She named him Joseph after my father, so we sometimes called him "Junior."

He slept in bed with Dad and Mamie until he was five years old, and was still sucking a bottle. He ate with Mamie and she carried him everywhere she went. He could do absolutely nothing for himself.

Behind Mamie's back, we used to tease him mercilessly by singing to him, "Mama's boy, Mama's boy, Suck your little titty."

Finally, when he was six, he begged Dad to tell Mamie to let him sleep in his own room. And Mamie, who always gave Stolen Boy whatever he wanted, reluctantly agreed.

I got my first beating because of Stolen Boy. I was in my room, sitting on the floor, when he came in and pulled my hair. Maybe he was just trying to be playful, but my immediate reaction was to push him away. I pushed with a little more force than I had intended, and he flew across the room, hit his head on the door, and started crying.

Hearing his cries, Mamie tore into the room and swept him away.

"What did she *do* to you?" I heard her say.

A moment later, she came back into my room with the extension cord.

"Lay across the bed!" she commanded.

I just sat there, looking shocked. At Mother's house, one of us was always pushing someone else around, and all Mother did about it was make us apologize or kiss each other.

Furious that I didn't immediately obey her, Mamie dragged me to the bed and shoved me face-down. Then she started beating me with the cord. Every lick made me hate her more. And I hated Stolen Boy, too, more than I thought possible.

When the lashings finally ended, I still hated her. But how could I hate Stolen Boy? He was standing in the doorway with his eyes locked on mine. His pain seemed to be far greater than what I was feeling from Mamie's hands. He looked so pitiful, standing there with his huge sad doe eyes. But he also looked ridiculous in the clothes Mamie put on him: high water overalls, white tube socks, and black and white oxfords. His breathing was weak, barely enough to fill his lungs with the emotionally polluted air that filled that house. He was saddened by the beating and embarrassed to be its cause.

As I looked at him, I began to cry—not from the beating I had just endured, but from the sorrow I saw in his eyes. For that moment, he was no longer Stolen Boy. He was Joseph.

On top of all our individual chores, we all had to take care of Joseph. Dressing him, combing his hair, brushing his teeth, and washing his butt were part of our daily routine. The only thing he did for himself was breathe, and that was shallow and pitiful. He became the saddest thing around that place next to the abuse we endured day after day.

How lonely he must have felt to live in a home full of siblings who would not talk to him or play with him—unless Mamie ordered us to. We all had each other. He only had Mamie. That was his own private hell.

"Do you take your coffee black ma'am?" the stewardess asked.

"Oh! I'm sorry. I didn't realize I asked for coffee," I responded, pulling down the tray in front of me.

"You seem a million miles away," she said. "Are you going on vacation?"

My response startled even me.

"No," I said, shaking my head. "This is no vacation. I have a date with the devil!"

As the stewardess walked away with a puzzled look on her face, I thought about my first real vacation.

It was the summer after I had moved in with Dad and Mamie. Joyce, Pat, Walter, and I were so excited because we would have two and a half months away from Mamie and the constant fear of beatings and humiliation.

When Dad pulled the car to the front of the house, I ran outside and began to spin in happy circles, swinging my arms with my head back. Just as I was about to let out a scream of joy, I was snatched by a powerful arm. Looking up, I jerked away, annoyed. It was Joyce, and she was destroying the moment for me. Grabbing my arm, she pulled me over toward the bushes on the side of the house, where the others were already huddled.

Everyone began scolding me.

"Are you out of your mind?" Pat yelled. It was not really a question. "We're not out of her reach yet! She'll find something to beat us about! She really doesn't want us to go and will find a reason to make us stay with her for the whole summer!"

That was the worst threat of all.

Joyce tried to soften the criticism that was being hurled at me.

"It's okay, Pat," she said. "She didn't know."

Tears began to well up in my eyes.

Mamie called out for us.

"Wipe your eyes!" Pat snapped at me. And reaching down, she took the hem of my dress and began dabbing my eyes.

Joyce frantically fanned my face to remove all traces of the tears.

We just stood there looking at each other. What could we do?

Walter immediately took over by plucking a few gardenias from a tree.

"Mama," he said, marching in front of us, "we wanted to give you something because we knew you would miss us."

As he handed her the flowers, she mumbled some superficial thanks. But that didn't matter. She had fallen for his ploy.

I followed the others' lead, putting my head down, pretending to be sad that we were leaving.

As we pulled away, Mamie consoled Joseph, who was sad because he couldn't come with us. But Mamie would never have allowed that, she was afraid that we would have killed him. He just stood there, waving sadly to us from the doorway.

As we drove away, I was excited to be leaving Portsmouth, a small town, bordering Norfolk, which is where the Navy base was. Developers had just discovered Portsmouth and were putting new buildings up all over town. We lived in one of the newest developments, called Cavalier Manor. Dad had bought a four-bedroom house on a corner lot for twelve thousand dollars. I looked out the window at all the new homes, most of them made of brick with attached garages. It was easy to get lost because all the houses looked so similar. The streets were clean and tidy, which is why I'm sure Mamie fell in love with the place.

Dad took us on the scenic route through town, so I saw more of Portsmouth that day than I had seen in the whole previous month. Our lives basically consisted of walking back and forth to school. Mamie rarely allowed us to go anywhere. When we did go out, it was usually to the church in North Carolina or with Dad to the Navy base in Norfolk.

I loved that base. It was so soothing to sit out by the water, watching the ships docking in or sailing out. When the sailors shipped out to sea, they would all line up on the top deck, dressed in their immaculate white uniforms, and stand at attention saluting until they were out of sight. The first time I saw Dad sail away like that, I was mesmerized, watching the sailors gradually turn into little toy men.

Once we got out of town, Dad played guessing games with us to pass the time. We never got to do that when Mamie was around. We stopped for lunch at a Dairy Queen, munching on burgers and fries, washing it all down with root beer floats. I had forgotten what those things tasted like. It had been nine months since I had left Boston and life as I had known it with Mom. My diet in Mamie's house was made up of a steady course of beans, Monday through Friday. On Saturdays, we were allowed to have hot dogs and pork and beans. On Sundays, we were finally blessed with a beanless meal—usually meatloaf or smothered chicken and cabbage.

A little after leaving the Dairy Queen, I needed to use a rest room, so Dad stopped on the side of the road.

"Go behind that tree," he said, pointing to a huge scary-looking oak a little ways off.

My eyes got so big with fright, looking at that old tree, squirming in my seat, I said, "That's all right, I can hold it."

"Come on!" Pat ordered, grabbing my hand and pulling me out of the car. "Why didn't you go while we were at the Dairy Queen?"

"I don't know."

As I was finishing up, I saw Pat walking away from the car to pick something up.

"What's that?" I hollered, too afraid to follow her.

"Just stay where you are," she yelled. Then she came running out of the woods with a bag in her hand, looking around as if someone were watching her. She shoved me in the car, and as Dad took off, she began to scream. She scared him so bad that he pulled over. We all looked at Pat in absolute amazement. She had a brown paper bag in her lap, and her hands were full of cash!

"I just found it," she exclaimed. "There were bills lying around, and as I began to pick them up, I saw this bag full of money."

Dad counted the money out, handing each one of us a portion. "This will be our secret," he said. "Don't tell anyone."

We all agreed, knowing perfectly well he meant Mamie.

3

Summer of Relief

When my father was five years old, his mother gave him to her sister, Minnie, who raised him. Aunt Minnie had no children of her own. We never knew why, and as far as I could remember, she never got married. Aunt Minnie was more like a grandmother to us than an aunt. She always remembered birthdays and holidays, although I can never recall her coming to our house. She and Mamie had no love for one another, and Minnie often voiced her disapproval of Dad's marriage.

As the car pulled up to Aunt Minnie's house, I saw the largest weeping willow I had ever seen, with a swing for two hanging from it, made from an old bench. Stepping out of the car, I just stood there gazing at that tree and the swing. With the sun beaming through the branches, it was the most peaceful scene I had ever experienced.

The slam of the screen door broke my gaze. Looking up, I saw a short round lady with a flawless smile. Her salt-and-pepper hair was pulled up into a bun.

Dad ran up to her, lifted her up in the air, and swung her around. Just as she landed on her feet, she looked into my eyes.

"Do you know who I am, baby?" she asked. And without waiting for a reply, she said, "I'm your Aunt Minnie."

Looking at Dad, she began to shake her head.

"She's all bones," she said.

At the time, I was five feet tall, but only weighed seventy pounds.

"They're *all* skinny as bones. What's that woman feeding them?"

Dad looked uncomfortable, but said nothing.

Sensing the anxiety on all our faces, Aunt Minnie started hugging us. "Just you wait," she said. "I'll have you good and fat in a couple of months when your dad comes to get you. You'll all be plump little turkeys."

She said that with her signature giggle.

As the airplane hit an air pocket, I was abruptly hurled back into the present. Looking around, I began to wonder how long we had been flying. Checking my watch, I realized that it had only been thirty minutes. This was going to be a long flight, not even counting the stopover in Denver. I was in dire need of a distraction. Flipping through the pages of a *Modern Home* magazine, the reality that everything I was and everything I wanted to be—or refused to become—was directly influenced by my past.

I thought about how Mamie and Aunt Minnie were as different as night and day. Mamie wanted everything modern, from the house she lived in to the furniture. Our car had to be the latest model and the brightest color. Her clothes were the latest fashion, even if she looked absurd in them. Everything about her was gaudy—all gold and glitter. Her taste was cheap and offensive. Consequently, my father was in endless debt, trying to please her. Her modern appliances were only for display. Mamie's obsession for perfection wouldn't allow her to use those lavish possessions, only to show them off. Of course, we were her possessions, too. People would often compliment her on how well-behaved we were, and she took great pride in hearing that the house was so immaculate that they couldn't believe children lived there. The fact is, we *didn't* live there. We were just another of her possessions.

I would stand there like a figurine in a glass house, pleading in my head to the visitors, "Please see me! Look closer. Please look into my eyes, and you'll see the pain just below the surface. I'm not living here. Break the glass and you'll expose the evil that's causing the pain."

But they would never look. Instead, I heard quaint comments. "Her eyes are so sad, like little puppy dogs."

"They're so fortunate you're here to help raise them, Mamie."

The superficial compliments would go on and on. Often we would smile, pretending to be grateful. We didn't live in a home, it was a house, and everything in it was cold and abrasive. There was no life anywhere. All the plants were artificial, and most of the furniture was wrapped in plastic. The drapes were heavy and formal, adorned with gold and white flowers and lots of pleats and folds like those in a mortuary.

The living room furniture was French provincial—maple-colored wood with gold flower prints on the fabric. There were two large gold lamps on both end-tables, and above the sofa hung a huge gold mirror. The dining room had a large table with chairs and a china cabinet that stretched the entire length of the wall. It was filled with Mamie's treasures, which included cups and saucers that she had collected from Dad's travels.

Our bedrooms were sparse, with only a bed and a dresser in each one. That made it easier to dust the rooms and harder to hide anything from Mamie.

In her own bedroom, there was a bed that was too big for the room, with a nightstand on either side. Across from the bed, there was a large dresser with a mirror attached, and above the bed there was a giant photograph of Mamie as a young woman.

All the floors in the house were hardwood with no rugs, and the flashy accessories were all too big for the rooms they were crammed into. The house smelled of disinfectants and cleaning solutions. Ammonia was everywhere.

Aunt Minnie's home was just the opposite. A huge porch wrapped halfway around the house, with white wicker chairs and tables on one side and a loveseat swing on the opposite side. Real ivy was hanging everywhere, and flowers and vegetables were growing freely in open containers. Morning glories with purple blooms were crawling up the porch. The house was filled with oversized chairs and sofas. Handmade doilies and recently dried flowers graced the tables.

My favorite room was the kitchen. The cabinets were not nearly as modern as those at Mamie's house, and they were all painted off-white. The tops of the cabinets were overflowing with knickknacks, mixing bowls, and various odds and ends. There was a large window over the sink, in which the sun streamed through with strings of herbs hanging to dry. The pantry held wall-to-wall homemade canned goods and baking supplies.

We often sat at the round table in the middle of the kitchen. Under the table, there was a multicolored rug that was almost like a homemade quilt. The kitchen was warmed by an old black pot belly wood-burning stove that stood in one corner of the room. Food was plentiful, and the aroma of fresh-baked pies or cakes often floated throughout the house. Most meals were prepared with fresh vegetables from the garden, where I would spend endless hours with Aunt Minnie..

My past had indeed dictated who and what I was. Already, I was missing Larry and the children. They were my safe haven. My home was filled with comfortable sofas and chairs, just like Aunt Minnie's.

I smiled as I remembered Larry's confusion when we purchased two sofas for our living room. Within months of bringing them home, I gave both of them away when I found a perfect sofa at a secondhand store. I adored that sofa, although it was a fraction of the cost of the others. They were too perfect and not at all inviting. Every time I walked through the living room, they reminded me of Mamie.

I loved plants and put fresh flowers throughout my house every week. The older an item was, the more fascinated I was with it. I taught my children the beauty of simple things.

There was such stillness and a sense of security when we were with Aunt Minnie. Our summers at her house were filled with long hot days and exciting nights.

A few days after we arrived, that first summer, I met Melissa and Marshall, a sister and brother who were visiting their grandmother,

Miss Pearl, across the road. Each morning, I was eager for the day to begin, absorbing every moment of my newfound freedom. Every day was filled with new adventures: gardening with Aunt Minnie, going to movies with my sisters, or exploring the neighborhood with my new friends. Melissa and I were both twelve. Marshall was almost fourteen. He spent a lot of time with Walter. I had never seen my brother happier. There was no sign of the anger that he would carry with him to school every day.

Our nine weeks of freedom in the summertime were like heaven. Pat and Joyce would get summer jobs at the market in town. Of course, Mamie was not to know anything about that, or she would take their money. Aunt Minnie pretended to buy all of us school clothes, but actually she only had to buy them for me, since I was the only one who didn't work. Walter shared a paper rout with Marshall.

Sunday morning breakfast was always full of chitchat. Aunt Minnie would prepare fresh squeezed orange juice and homemade biscuits, which just melted in your mouth. One Sunday, Melissa and Marshall were over as usual, when suddenly the phone rang. Since it didn't ring very often, we all stopped talking and looked around at one another. No one wanted to answer the phone because it felt like a premonition. Finally, Joyce walked over and picked up the receiver.

In a weak voice, she began to plead, "No, two weeks, not one! Yes, sir. Okay, Dad."

Hanging up the phone and trying to camouflage her disappointment, she said, almost in a whisper, "We'll be returning home a week earlier. Mamie wants us to be ready for school."

Tears welled up in my eyes. I was always the first to cry, and I disliked that about myself.

The mood in the room sank to an all-time low.

Aunt Minnie chuckled as she walked around the room, hugging each of us.

"Let's make this the longest week in the year," she said. "Eat up! We've got lots to do."

We all agreed. We couldn't delay the inevitable, but we could dismiss it for a while. Each of us agreed not to speak about our departure. We decided to cram as much fun into the next week as possible.

Melissa and I literally became blood sisters, vowing to meet every summer at the same time and never to lose contact with each other. We promised to name our children after each other and grow old together, maybe even move to the same town. She promised to write often. Understanding my situation, she knew I would not be permitted to write back.

Joyce and Pat had summer boyfriends and were always going to the show or out to lunch with other teenagers when they weren't at work. Walter and Marshall could always be found playing basketball at the park or fishing at the lake. Marshall had asked me to be his girlfriend, and I had agreed, but we were seldom alone together. Most of the time, we were with Walter and Melissa. Aunt Minnie was always busy making us pajamas, knitting scarves for the coming winter, or baking one of her homemade pies. In other words, with Mamie out of the picture, our lives were pretty normal.

I shared my last evening that first summer with Melissa, who tried everything to keep my mind occupied. We filled the night with playing board games, Truth or Dare, and dressing up in old clothes that we found in Aunt Minnie's attic, which was as magical and enchanting as she was. It was filled with old clothes and fancy hats from her younger days. I would often hide out up there, trying on outfits and pretending to be someone else. Melissa and I would have tea parties up there, losing ourselves in the past.

On this last evening, Melissa spent the night, and I could tell she could sense my dread. I had shared with her that *Heidi* was one of my favorite stories, so she began to tell her version of the story, changing the names of the characters to ours. She said the mean old stepmother would die, and her parents would come and get me, and we would be sisters, living happily ever after.

"Promise me that you will believe this," she said. "Just say over and over again that we will be sisters for life."

Soon we fell asleep.

The heat from the morning sun beaming on my face woke me the next morning. To my astonishment, Melissa had already gone. I jumped up and ran to the bathroom. The nausea was back. My stomach was in knots, and I began to heave involuntarily. I threw cold water on my face and chanted repeatedly, "Relax! Calm down!" After a few moments, the nausea began to subside. I sat through breakfast, but I couldn't eat a thing.

Aunt Minnie never said a word. Her eyes did all the talking as she held my hand.

Looking at the clock, I saw that I had just enough time to say goodbye to Melissa and Marshall. I ran across the road, but before I could knock on the door, it swung open. Melissa was standing with a strange look on her face, as Marshall came up behind her. Glancing down, I recognized my suitcase.

"Hey," I said, "how did this get here?"

Shifting back and forth, Marshall said, "Your brother got something stuck in the zipper. I had to get pliers to repair it."

"I've gotta go," I said, picking up my suitcase.

The three of us began to run to Aunt Minnie's house. But just before we got to the high hedge that bordered their yard, I heard Mamie's voice across the road.

Looking down at the suitcase, I yelled, "Oh, God! She'll think I was staying over here. I'm not allowed to sleep over, *ever*. I'll never be able to come back!"

Walter appeared out of nowhere. I pointed to the suitcase. There was no need for words. Our survival was based on being able to read each other's minds. Grabbing the suitcase, he motioned for Melissa and me to go on.

Running out to the car, trying to dismiss my anxiety, I greeted Mamie and Dad with a hug.

With precise timing, Marshall ran up to shake their hands, exclaiming, "I've heard so much about you. Walter's my best friend. Can you please come over and meet our grandmother?"

Not waiting for an answer, he grabbed Mamie's hand and guided her to the door, as Dad followed behind.

"You have soft hands, like my mother" he whispered with a little wink. Marshall was such a charmer, talking and diverting Mamie's attention.

The moment they were out of sight, Walter came running up with my suitcase.

It was agonizing to have to say goodbye to Aunt Minnie.

I was usually forced to take the middle seat in the front, but Joseph was there, so Joyce let me have her seat by the back window. Recognizing how distraught I was about leaving, she was afraid I might expose my grief.

I took my sweater off and covered my face with it, pretending to be asleep. Soon my body began to shake reluctantly as a flood of tears began streaming down my face.

Why is this happening? Can I survive another year of this torment?

The silent tears turned to sobs.

Joyce quickly put her hand over my mouth.

Before leaving town, Dad pulled into a gas station. Joyce grabbed me and pulled me to the rest room.

"You can't continue this!" she scolded. "She'll beat the hell out of you! Wash your face!"

Suddenly, without warning, the walls began to close in on me. The room was turning.

I began to scream, "I want my mother! I just wanna go home! Help me, please!" I was begging now. "Joyce, you must help me contact Mother."

Seeing the bewilderment on my face and trying to quiet my outburst, she agreed.

"Okay! Okay!" she said, close to tears. "When I write a letter for Mamie, I'll steal a stamp. Do you remember Mother's address?"

"Yes, I know it," I murmured. "Ninety West Cottage Street."

I suddenly had a glimpse of hope.

As we got back in the car, Joyce casually announced, "Just another one of her nausea episodes. Maybe it's the long ride."

The remainder of the ride home was less stressful as I thought about my life in Boston and my longing to return there. It was so different. There I was the oldest, not the youngest, because Mother had remarried and I had five younger siblings.

Mother was a nurse at the county hospital. She left for work every weekday at four in the afternoon, so we were home at night with my stepfather. It was a little harder for me now that Granny was gone, because my stepfather had free reign over me. But I could deal with that. I was thinking I would just reveal the whole truth to Mother.

Usually, Mother would cook dinner before she left for work. If not, I would make hot dogs, sandwiches, or leftovers. After bathing and doing homework, everyone went to bed at nine. My favorite times were reading to my younger siblings. Looking back, life was so simple then.

Granny used to prepare all the meals and take care of the younger children, but she died about a year before I moved in with my dad. After Granny died, I was given more responsibilities. Granny's death was very hard on Mother. She was the youngest of nine children, but Granny lived with us as long as I can remember. She was my mother's right arm. I felt so guilty when Granny died, because I hadn't believed that she was sick.

She was a very small-framed woman with long wavy black hair and the most beautiful gray streak right down the middle of her head. Granny would just mosey around the house until it was time for the doctor to come. Shortly before he arrived, she would take a bath, put on her nightgown, and lie down in bed to wait for him. Usually, he left her a lot of medications and prescriptions, and the moment he was gone she would jump out of bed, get dressed, and go about her daily routines.

This time was different. He called an ambulance to take Granny to the hospital. Two days later, Mother was crying. I overheard her talking with Grace. Granny had died in her sleep. Existing in a state of denial, until the day of her funeral, I kept waiting for Granny to come through the door. She never did.

Mother always told us about our older siblings, but we were so young when they left, we didn't remember them. Then, one day, she told us that they were coming to spend the whole summer with us! All my friends would finally see that I wasn't making up stories about my older brother and sisters.

As I thought about that summer, looking out the window of the car, it hit me. Did I leave, or was I ripped from my mother? It had been more than a year, and there had been no phone calls or letters. Back in Boston, Mother was always in constant contact with us. If she was going to be late coming home from work, she would call and reassure us she was fine.

My mind began to roam back to the day I left Boston. I was introducing my older siblings to all my friends. We had cousins over who had never met my older siblings. Without notice, only a week after their arrival, Dad appeared with Mamie, and there was a great deal of tension in the house. Dad told me I was leaving with him. Then he called Mother at the hospital and told her. I didn't know what to do.

Pat walked between my father and me, motioning something with her hands that I didn't understand.

Then Walter grabbed me and gave me a hug. "Stay here!" he whispered. "Don't come!" Then, stepping away from me, he blurted out, "I'm gonna miss ya!"

Not understanding what they were trying to tell me, I wanted to go with them for a visit.

"Can I come back?" I asked Dad.

Without answering me, he said into the phone, "She's going with me." He said this very bitterly.

Everyone was crying as they quickly packed their bags.

Then the police arrived as we were going out the front door.

Dad showed them some papers, and off we went.

"Wake up! We're home!"

It was Joyce, shaking me into the present.

If I can just get a letter to Mother, everything will be fine.

The day Dad and Mamie picked us up at Aunt Minnie's was a Sunday. Mamie, who couldn't read or write, usually had Joyce write letters for her on Friday evenings. That evening I rushed to bed, thinking about the coming Friday. Then I wondered why I hadn't tried to contact Mother all summer, when I had the opportunity. Instead, I was busy having fun, pretending this day would never come. That night I decided that I could no longer afford the luxury of being a naive child. I had to help get us out of this terrible condition. The situation we were in was insane. But the insanity climaxed our will to survive and became a driving force in our life.

The following morning, it became clear why we were rushed from Aunt Minnie's house. Dad was packed and saying his goodbyes. His ship was sailing out early. It wasn't about us being prepared for school at all. Queen Mamie needed her personal servants at home on duty.

Usually when my father left, I carried on so pathetically that Mamie sent me to bed. Not this time. I grieved a little, but my main focus was getting a letter to Mother.

Friday came, and just as Joyce had promised, she was able to sneak a stamp. Getting paper would have to wait a few days until school started. Mamie gave each of us a three-ring binder with a separator between each of our classes. If we needed more paper, we had to show her that our paper was used for assignments. If they weren't, we were punished. This usually consisted of a beating or maybe no lunch for a week—whatever suited her fancy. In fact, under Mamie's rule, our *whole life* was a punishment. We were never allowed to watch television or use the telephone. Every day consisted of cleaning and waiting on her and Joseph, hand and foot. Of course, we had to do our homework, but that was only to impress the teachers about how well parented we were.

When she got a chance, Joyce counted out the paper so that Mamie could hear it, but she slipped two extra sheets into my binder when Mamie turned her head. That night I was so excited that I forgot I had lunch duty.

Joyce rushed into my room.

"Get in there and do lunch duty while she's still in the bath!" she scolded.

I ran to the kitchen and began making sandwiches. Sometimes, I made peanut butter and jelly. Other times, it was baloney. Every night, Mamie would check our lunch bags, making sure that our sandwiches were very thin. With the baloney we were allowed no condiments, just two slices of dry bread and one thin slice of meat. She gave each of us a sandwich bag at the beginning of the week and one sheet of wax paper. If we lost the bag, we went without lunch until the following week. I was so embarrassed about having to save the bag and the paper that I would fold them up and slip them into one of my books when no one was watching. Mamie gave us each ten cents a day for milk. But then she would often take this away if our bags were too wrinkled or anything else bothered her.

The next day, I wrote Mother a letter, telling her about some of the terrible conditions we had to live under and begging her to come and get me.

Joyce warned me not to put a return address on the envelope, in case I had the wrong address and the letter came back. Although I was certain of Mother's address, I followed her advice.

The hard part was getting the letter to the mailbox. The closest one was eight blocks from school. Walter had me walk at my normal pace on the way home, while he ran to the mailbox and caught up with me in just enough time for us to reach the corner together. There was no room for error. Mamie usually would be at the window watching out for us.

The following few weeks went by without any confrontations with Mamie. Then, one day, while Pat was trying to get a project done for homework, she got distracted and burned a pot of beans.

The rest of us kids were sitting at the dinner table in the garage, wondering what we were going to eat, since we could smell the burning beans throughout the house.

When Mamie saw those beans, she made Pat put them on a plate and carry them to the dining table.

When Pat put the plate down on the table, Mamie said, "Now, eat!"

Pat took a few bites, thinking that would satisfy her. But it was not enough. Striking her on the head, Mamie ordered, "The whole plate! Otherwise you'll get a beating!"

As Pat put a few more beans into her mouth, Mamie left the room.

Suddenly, Pat started vomiting all over her plate.

We all ran up to her to console her, and Walter scraped the beans and vomit into a trash can.

Mamie returned with the extension cord and began swinging it wildly against Pat.

Pat fell to the floor, receiving the blows until Mamie was exhausted.

Thank God, it's over! I thought.

Mamie told Pat to get up and wash her face. I was wondering

what we were going to eat ourselves that night, now that the dinner was burned.

When Pat came back from the bathroom, Mamie pointed to the beans and said, "Eat!"

"No!"

Pointing to us, Mamie said, "Go to bed. And *you*," indicating Pat, "will sit at that table all night until you're ready to eat."

At four o'clock in the morning, Mamie ran around the house, shouting to all of us, "Get up! Go to the garage! Now!"

When I got there, I could barely focus because my eyes felt like they had glass pebbles in them. But I could see well enough to tell that Pat was still awake and now sitting at the table in the garage. Her body was slumped over, and she could hardly keep her eyes open.

Mamie said, "She's ready to eat now."

Joyce picked up Pat's plate to get her some more burned beans.

"Put down that plate!" Mamie commanded.

Then she grabbed the plate from Joyce, walked over to the trash can, scooped out the beans and vomit, and sat it in front of Pat.

Tears streamed down Pat's face as she picked up the spoon and began to eat.

Without warning, I began to heave violently. Next thing I knew, urine was running down my legs.

"Clean up that mess and go to bed!" Mamie screamed, and stormed up to her bedroom.

Joyce rushed over to help me, and Walter helped Pat to clean up.

That night, something innocent inside me died. Hatred began to creep into my heart. Pulling the blanket over my head, I tried to hide the ugliness that was growing inside my heart. I just wanted Mamie dead.

4

Still Life

A few weeks later, when Dad was back from sea, Joyce walked in one day and gave Mamie the mail. Then she signaled me to come out to the garage. Seeing all this, Pat followed us.

"What is it?" I whispered.

"A letter from Mother to Dad."

I was thrilled.

"Can I see it?"

"I had to give it to her. Now, don't act any different, or she'll know I went through the mail."

We waited for three days. Every Saturday, Dad would drive Mamie and Joseph an hour away to Elizabeth City to see Mamie's sister, Beatrice. "Aunt Bea" was a lot nicer than Mamie and sometimes stood up for us, not that Mamie listened to her. On those Saturdays, Mamie would stay away all day, shopping, and visiting other relatives. Dad would go and visit Aunt Minnie or do some work at our church, the Bethel Church of God in Christ, in Elizabeth City. He was a close friend of the pastor, who had known him since Dad was a boy.

Joyce, Pat, Walter, and I worked out a perfect routine for Saturdays. First, we would wait for fifteen minutes to make sure they wouldn't be returning. Then we would watch TV, or call our friends, or make something special to eat. I was already a coffee addict, from drinking it with my grandmother in Boston, so I would brew myself a delicious pot of coffee.

On this particular Saturday, once we were sure they were gone, we all began searching Mamie's room, making sure we placed everything back precisely where she had left it. Mamie was menacingly paranoid and would often leave markers alerting her that something was out of place.

Suddenly, Walter exclaimed, "I've got it!"

We all jumped on the bed. My heart was beating so fast. The letter was short and to the point. Mother had a vacation coming in three weeks and would be in town for six days. She was planning on getting a hotel room and wanted us to stay with her a few days. All the flight information was in the letter.

I began jumping, screaming, and running around the room. I had such an overwhelming sense of joy. The others were more reserved. Puzzled by this, I abruptly stopped my rejoicing.

"What's wrong?" I asked.

"Mother can only do so much," Joyce said. "After a few days, she'll leave, and we'll continue to live in misery, paying for revealing the truth to her. Dad has custody of us."

"I can't stay here any longer!" I blurted out. "You don't *know* Mother. She would never let anyone mistreat her children. I've seen her fight for her kids. She would never leave us once she knows the truth."

I was certain of this, and one by one I gradually won them over.

We devised a plan that night. I would simply tell Mother I wanted to go back home because I missed her and my younger siblings so much, and I could not wait for the moment we would be able to talk freely. I would reveal the abuse and mistreatment we were receiving. Our strategy was so simple, I was filled with enthusiasm. My siblings, on the other hand, were reserved.

At first, I was a little troubled by this, but I began to think of all the years of abuse and disappointment they had suffered. And after all, they didn't really know Mother. They were taken away from her so young that their memories of her were totally distorted.

The following two weeks were nerve-wracking. There was no mention of Mother's arrival. As soon as Dad left for his weekend duty, Mamie gathered us in the garage.

"We'll be having a house guest," she announced smugly.

"A house guest!" I said. "Who is it?"

"You'll know soon enough," she said. "And there will be a price to pay if anyone opens their mouth!"

I was so excited that I thought I would burst. We had never had a house guest before, so it had to be Mother! In just a few days, she would be here, and I could tell her all the horrible things that were going on. I was so confident she would fix the whole situation that I began to make plans for our departure.

The weekend that Mother was to arrive finally came. Of course, the house was spotless, one of the bedrooms was prepared for her, and clean pressed linen was put on every bed. A basket full of brand-new towels was placed in the bedroom prepared for Mother, and for the first time, we were given new towels to bathe with.

Dad and Mamie left for the airport, and we kids sat in the dark, waiting for our house guest.

Suddenly, the car lights hit the wall, and we heard the car doors slam. Before Dad could get his key in the lock, I pulled the door open. Mother was standing there. I lunged into her arms, and all the emotions I had experienced for the last year and a half swept over me. I began to sob like a broken animal.

"Give your mother a chance!" Mamie scolded.

Mother looked at her and said, "Surely, you realize she's been away from me for such an extended period of time."

With that she sat on the floor in the living room and began to rock me back and forth. The others were just standing there. Finally, Mother motioned for them to join us, and each one ran to her, hugging her as if she had simply been on vacation. We were there on the floor for over an hour. Dad and Mamie had disappeared into their bedroom. Mother had a million questions, and she began to tell us all about our younger siblings. I asked her about my friends and my old school. Oh, how I longed to go back to life as I had known it.

Suddenly, Mamie interrupted us with an agitated look on her face.

"Maybe you should let your mother get settled," she proclaimed, and rushed out of the room.

Mother looked at us reassuringly and got up, following Mamie to the room that was prepared for her. Dad was already there, sitting in a chair. As Mother walked in, Mamie closed the door behind her.

We all stood at the door, listening. Mamie began by telling

Mother how much of a burden it was to raise her four children, and how blessed my father was to have her, because what single woman would give up her life to raise another woman's children? What followed shocked us all. Apparently, the courts had given my father full custody of all my siblings while my mother was still pregnant with me. Mamie went on to explain that everyone, including our close friends and teachers, thought she was our real mother. To avoid any questions, Mamie said she had simply told everyone that Mother was her half-sister. We would be instructed to call her our Aunt in public.

We could only hear a whisper come from Mother.

"Vernon," she said, calling him by the middle name she always used. "Vernon..." Her voice was trembling as she choked back tears.

"Dee..." Dad said. Her name was Delores, but Dad always called her Dee. "Dee, I'm only home six months out of the year. What would you have me do with them when I'm gone?"

"Give them back."

"That's out of the question. Not as long as..."

"Not as long as what?" I asked Joyce. "What is he saying?"

Joyce shrugged.

Then we heard steps, and ran to the front of the house. Mamie came into the living room and declared, "You will call her your Aunt in public. I'm raising you, and I am your mother."

That night, while Mamie was asleep, I crept out of bed and went into the hallway. As I passed Joyce and Pat's bedroom, Joyce whispered, "Where are you going?"

Pat popped up in her bed, and Walter appeared at the door of his bedroom. No one's door was allowed to be closed—except Mamie's, of course. I looked at them all, wondering what they were thinking.

"I'm gonna sleep with Mother."

They looked so puzzled, but didn't say another word.

I opened Mother's door. She was waiting for me, and I crawled into bed with her. Mother and I both cried without saying a word. Memories began flooding in of being home with Grandma cooking, and Mother coming home from work and sitting down to rest on the sofa. She would listen to each of us telling her how our day had gone. On the weekends, we all slept with Mother or Grandma. There were bodies all over the bed.

Around 6:00 a.m. the next morning, Joyce knocked on the door and came in. Mother motioned for her to sit on the bed. "You're up so early," Mother said.

"We have to do our chores, and then we'll come back."

Joyce signaled me to come with her. When we were out in the hall, she took me by the hand and led me quickly out to the garage, where Pat and Walter were waiting. They all began to bombard me with questions.

"Did you say anything?"

"Mother let you sleep with her?"

"Was she angry?"

"It's normal for kids to sleep with their mother," I said. "Remember how I used to tell you stories about how we would have slumber parties with Mother and Grandma before she passed?"

Looking at my siblings, I realized for the first time that they had been deprived of so much. "Mother would love to have all of you sleep with her," I said. "You can't compare her with Mamie. She *loves* you! She gave birth to you. No matter what Mamie told you in the past, Mother did *not* give you up willingly. I'm certain she was forced."

The next few days were so peaceful. We were all on our best behavior. We all slept in Mother's room the entire time she was with us, taking turns sleeping on the floor. It was so much fun to watch Joyce and Pat interact with Mother. She told them how beautiful and smart they were. It was praise that neither of them was used to receiving.

Walter was a perfect gentleman. He wouldn't sleep in bed with Mother, but he picked her fresh flowers and would bring her coffee every morning.

Eventually, I got an opportunity to tell Mother that I was planning to go back home with her.

"I'm homesick," I said, "and I miss my younger brothers and sisters."

Mother had a confused look on her face.

"I tried to get your father to send you home months ago," she said. "The kids are having a hard time adjusting to Grandma's death and your leaving. I'm sure you're not adjusting very well, either."

"Dad never told me that he talked to you," I said. "When you didn't respond to my letters, I thought maybe you didn't want me to come home."

"I'll deal with your dad," she said. "Of course, you can come home. I have custody of you!"

As soon as I could get the others alone, I told them about my conversation with Mother, and how she had tried to get Dad to send me home. Finally, I saw a glimpse of hope.

Pat began to make plans with me for my departure. She even packed my suitcase for me, which I hid under my bed.

That Saturday, we went to the town carnival. It was my first time at a carnival since I had left Boston. Mother used to take us every year. It was one of her favorite pastimes.

Walter was so excited. He kept disappearing and coming back with large stuffed animals. He had one for each of us.

And I had never seen Pat laugh so much. She had the most beautiful white teeth. In Mamie's house, she was so angry all the time. It was a rare occasion to see her smile.

That evening, we all sat in Mother's room, telling her about our summer with Aunt Minnie and our friends. For the first time, Mother explained to us that she wanted all her children at home with her, but there were legal issues. She was sure she still had custody of me, because she and Dad had not been to court since I was born. That was settled. She would tell him in the morning that I was leaving with her.

That night, I was so excited I could hardly sleep. Joyce woke up me early the next morning so I could finish packing. After breakfast, Mother went into Dad and Mamie's bedroom. At first, you could barely hear a whisper. Then the voices became louder and louder. Finally, you could hear Mamie screaming. She was threatening to call the police, threatening to never let Mother see us again. Mother was pleading with Dad.

Finally, she came out of the room. I was standing there. The others had tried to pull me away, but I had refused to budge.

Mother looked down at me and said, "I'm sorry. I'll come back and get you."

"No, no!" I screamed. "I won't stay here another day!"

Within moments, Mother had her bag, and Dad was taking her to the airport.

I grabbed her bag and wouldn't let go.

"You have to take me!" I pleaded. "I'll die here!"

Mother was sobbing.

Walter pried my fingers from the suitcase and carried it to the car.

This was the first time I ever saw Walter be disrespectful to Dad. He looked at him and said with contempt, "Just go. I'll take care of Reesa."

Dad got in the car and began to drive away. I ran after the car, banging on the window. Then I slipped and fell. As I lay in the middle of the street with my nose bleeding and one shoe off, my brother came and picked me up and carried me to the house.

5

The Agenda

For weeks, I wouldn't speak. It didn't matter how many threats Mamie came up with. My siblings and Dad tried to bribe me, but I didn't say a single word for weeks. I tried, but there was too much grief.

Then one day, Mamie decided that she was going to force me to talk. She came into my room with the extension cord and ordered me to strip. As I did, tears were streaming down my face. I lay on the bed, and she began to whip me with the cord.

"You're just being stubborn," she said. "You better open your mouth and say something, or I'm not gonna stop till you do."

I tried. My mouth would form the words, but I had no voice. As the blows rained down on me, I lost track of time. Suddenly, my bedroom door flew open and it was Walter. He walked over to my bed and lay on top of me to shield me.

Mamie slung the cord at him, striking him over and over again. But he just lay there, accepting all the punishment intended for me. Finally, she retreated to her room. Standing up, he never turned to look at me. I could see his body trembling. Slowly he reached back to hand me my clothes and walked out of my room.

I tried to say thank you. The words were in my brain, but there was a disconnection. I had overdosed on the torment, and my soul was slowly and silently hemorrhaging.

A few weeks later, after hearing nothing from Mother, Walter decided that he could no longer tolerate our living conditions. He had to handle his pain the only way he knew how. He had heard about a traveling circus coming to town, and made up his mind to run away with it.

The circus's last day in town would be Halloween, a Friday night.

After everyone had settled down and gone to bed, Walter came in and gave us a hug. Joyce tried the last time in vain to persuade him to stay.

"At least take your sleeping bag," she said.

Walter agreed, and said, he'd contact Mother at the first opportunity he got.

On Saturday mornings, we were allowed to sleep until 8:00 a.m. At about 8:01 a.m., Pat marched into Mamie's room and revealed with total pleasure that Walter was not in his room and apparently hadn't slept there.

Mamie began to question us frantically. Then I heard her on the telephone, telling the police that Walter had behavioral problems. Her next call was to Aunt Minnie. Again, she put all the blame on Walter. Aunt Minnie was very concerned. Mamie told her that the police said he was not gone long enough to file a missing person's report. They felt he was just a troubled teenager and would eventually show up.

Every hour that passed was a milestone for us. We knew that the circus had left town at 6:00 p.m., which meant that he had been gone over ten hours. Pat kept asking Joyce what city he was in by now. We were so excited that Joyce had to keep scolding us.

"Pat," she warned, "if you don't be quiet, she'll hear you and call the police to go after him!"

That evening, we went to bed extremely optimistic because Walter had promised us that if he couldn't join the circus, he would call three times in a row and hang up after one ring. Since the phone calls never came, we figured he was gone long enough to be in another state.

On Sunday morning, we were up preparing for church when the telephone rang. We all stopped what we were doing when we heard Mamie say, "Yes, I'm his mother."

Her next response worried us.

"How bad is he?... I'll contact his father... he's away at sea."

Immediately after hanging up, she called the Coast Guard and told them that she had to get a message to Dad.

"His son's in the hospital in critical condition," she said.

We all began to cry. There were so many unanswered questions. Pat was fuming and began spewing out insults.

"It's all her fault! She's a witch from hell!"

Mamie pretended not to hear her.

As always, Joyce kept trying to calm Pat.

I needed to get away. Not caring what Mamie would do, I walked out the front door. I wanted to scream, but nothing came out. There was snow on the ground, but I lay down on my belly, feeling empty.

God, can you hear me? I began to pray in my head. *Father, please don't let my brother die!*

I don't know how long I lay there. I was crying without making a sound. After a little while, my fingers started getting stiff. I had left the front door wide open, so Mamie must have felt the chill coming in, because she looked out and saw me.

"Go get her," she said to Joyce. "She's going crazy."

Joyce came out and kneeled down by me, softly saying, "Reesa you have to pull it together."

I want to talk, but I just can't. I want to know how Walter is. I have a million questions for him. I was frustrated with myself because the words just wouldn't come.

Joyce helped me up and led me into the house. She took me by the hand to the bathroom and ran water in the tub. I undressed and climbed into the warm water. My fingers lost their stiffness, but my soul was still numb.

Sometime later, as I was walking out of the bathroom, a military car came by to pick Mamie up. Joyce, Pat, and I sat in a trance in the living room. We had totally forgotten that there was someone else in the house. Then we heard someone crying.

"I'll get him," Pat said. "He must be hungry."

"I'll fix him some dinner," Joyce said.

When Pat went to his room, I heard her say, "Are you worried about Walter, Joseph?"

"I want my mama!"

He was probably as shocked as we were that Mamie had left him behind.

When we all gathered in the kitchen, Joyce took a chicken out of the freezer.

"What are you doing?" Pat asked.

"We're *all* eating tonight!" Joyce said.

"And you're gonna keep your mouth shut about this," Pat said to Joseph.

So that night, we all got to eat in the kitchen, instead of the garage, and we ate meat instead of beans. But with Walter in the hospital, we hardly enjoyed a bite.

Mamie didn't come home until about 10:00 p.m. that evening

"Your dad's on his way home," she muttered. "Your brother really pulled a good one this time."

No one asked her how Walter was because we knew she wouldn't tell us anyway. But we searched her face for any clues. From what she said, we at least knew he was alive.

"Bea," she said into the phone to her sister, "can you come over here and pick up Joseph? Or send someone? I have to go back to the hospital."

When she got off the phone, she took a quick shower, changed her clothes, and left in the military car.

Around midnight, Aunt Bea's daughter, Jennifer, showed up at the door. Pat, who sometimes treated Joseph like her own baby, went to his bedroom, wrapped him in a blanket, and carried him out to the car.

Dad arrived home around 1:00 a.m. Without saying a word to us, he changed out of his uniform into civilian clothes and headed for the front door.

I was standing there with my back against the door, still unable to speak. I looked into his eyes for reassurance, but his gaze was as blank as mine.

He lifted my small frame out of his way.

"I'll call," he said, and closed the door in my face.

For the next hour, we just sat still, looking at each other watching the clock.

Suddenly, the phone rang.

Pat jumped up and answered it on the second ring. After a moment, her face dropped.

"Oh, hi, Aunt Minnie... You spoke to Dad?... Walter's gonna be okay? How does Dad know that?... No, for once Mamie didn't beat him. Walter was just so sad that we hadn't heard from Mother by now. He decided to run off with the circus. But we all thought he was okay because he hadn't signaled us. I guess we should have stopped him... Okay, call us if you hear anything."

When Pat hung up, Joyce scolded her. "You know we're not allowed to answer the phone when Mamie's not here."

"But Dad said he'd call."

"You didn't wait for the signal. You know they always ring twice, hang up, and call back."

Pat lashed out, "I don't give a damn about any signal when my brother's lying in the hospital half dead! I'm answering the damn phone, and I'll just take the beating!"

Then the telephone rang again. Pat immediately snatched it from the receiver.

"Hello?... Okay, we'll be ready."

As she hung up, she looked confused. Then, with a quivering voice, she said, "Dad's on his way to get us. He said to be ready."

In less than half an hour, Dad pulled up into the driveway. We all rushed out the door, not even waiting for him to honk the horn. Mamie wasn't with him, so I figured she was back at the hospital, playing the loving concerned mother.

Joyce got in the front seat, Pat, and I got in back.

"Dad, what happened?" Joyce asked.

"From what the police can piece together," Dad said, "your brother tried to join the circus. He told them his parents were dead, and he lived with relatives. The guy thought he was just another runaway and told him to come back in the morning. It appears that your brother slept outside one of the tents in his sleeping bag. It snowed that evening, and someone found him the next morning. When they tried to wake him up, he was unresponsive. The doctors say we have to wait it out. There could be brain damage or organ failure. But at this point, it's all just speculation. The only thing we know for sure right now is that he's in a coma and on life support."

Unresponsive! Coma! Life support!

I began to hyperventilate.

Knowing my history, Joyce opened the glove compartment, pulled out a brown paper bag, and handed it to Pat, who just snapped it open with one swift move and threw it at me. I took slow, deep breaths into the bag to calm down.

Pat was so bitter and angry, there was no room in her for compassion. She just sat there, twisting, turning, and grunting like a caged animal.

When we arrived at the military hospital, the intensive care unit doctors tried to prepare us for what we were about to encounter. I looked at Dad, but he wouldn't make eye contact. He was slumped over, looking weak and defeated.

Pat didn't wait for the doctors to finish. Turning to one of the nurses, she said, "Where's my brother?"

In response, the nurse motioned to a room at the far end of the corridor.

Pat bolted toward the room, as one of the doctors tried to catch up with her, to explain to her what she would see.

I ran behind them.

As Pat rushed into Walter's room, she stood immobilized, blocking the door. I stepped around her, took one look at Walter, and the room went black.

The next thing I knew, I was sitting up, pushing away a doctor's hand. Before he could speak, I remembered where I was. Nothing the doctors had said had prepared me for what I had just seen. Walter was lying lifeless with tubes coming from his mouth, chest, and left side. A machine was breathing for him. His complexion was dark and ashen, his lips and fingertips blue.

Suddenly, there was a commotion in the corridor and I jumped up. The voices were familiar. As I ran into the corridor, I saw Pat and Mamie confronting each other.

Pat turned to Dad and screamed, "You need to call Mother!"

Mamie screeched, "*I'm* his mother!"

"No, you're not!" Pat shouted.

With that, Mamie stepped back and with all her force brutally struck Pat across the face.

Pat's head jerked around involuntarily. You could hear a gasp from the nurses and doctors who were witnessing this scene.

Pat slowly turned back to face Mamie. You could see the rage in her eyes. The revulsion she felt was so thick it was tangible. "You never gave birth to *anything*!" she snarled.

Mamie slapped her again.

"Never!" Pat grunted.

Another, more forceful blow.

Blood began to flow from Pat's nose. She let it drip down her face, showing no emotion. For a moment, it seemed that everyone who was watching this battle was in a state of disbelief. Finally, a nurse ran up to Pat and put a towel over her nose and mouth.

After this incident, none of the nurses or doctors would look at us. Their glances were brief, as if the shame had somehow penetrated them.

"Take me home!" Mamie commanded my father.

"Let's go," he said to us.

"*No!*"

This was the first word I had spoken since Mother left. Tears were streaming down my face.

"Dad," I pleaded, "look at me. We can't all leave him."

He knew what I was saying. We were all asking a question that we were too afraid to say out loud, terrified that it might finalize his fate. Was he going to die?

A burst of courage came over me. "I'm not leaving," I said. "You'll have to drag me out of here."

Dad was surprised at my reaction and looked at the nurses.

The head nurse nodded as if it is alright for me to stay.

"Okay," Dad said. "I'll pick you up in the morning."

When all the visitors had left, the head nurse took me into the ICU waiting room, and gave me a blanket. I just lay there wide awake, thinking about my brother.

At some point in the middle of the night, one of the late-shift nurses came up to me.

"You can stay in the room with your brother," she said.

When we got there, I saw two lights set up on either side of Walter's bed, aimed at him.

"What are the lights for?" I asked.

"We're slowly trying to warm his body up."

"Can he hear us if he's in a coma?"

"Sometimes, the body is so sick that you lose too much energy if you're awake, so it's God's way of allowing the body to regenerate. But it's not uncommon for people to remember their loved ones talking to them when they come out of a coma."

There was a comfortable easy chair in the room. I sat on it, stretched out my legs, and waited till I was sure no one was out in the corridor. Then I crawled into bed with my brother and began to tell him the story of Helen Keller. Before long, we were talking to God together, spirit to spirit. I willed life to Walter. My greatest asset was my faith. Through all of this misery with Mamie, I still believed! But I needed Walter to believe, too.

As I fell asleep curled up next to my brother, I had the most serene dream. I was standing high on a ladder in the garage, when I suddenly lost my balance and began to fall. Just as I was panicking, I heard a voice say, "Relax." As I did, my body began to levitate. I rose above the room with a total sense of peace. Walter came in and saw me. I convinced him he could do it, too. He did.

The next morning, I felt a hand shaking me. Looking around, I realized I was in the hospital. Walter's eyes were open, and he was looking right at me!

Wanting to make sure he was alright, I ran out to the corridor to find a nurse. The one who had let me stay with Walter wasn't far away.

When we got back to his bed, she said to him, "Well, you're surely a miracle!"

She looked at his fingers, which now were pink. His lips formed a smile around the tube that was hanging from his mouth.

Walter pointed to the tube, indicating that he wanted it out.

"Just you wait a minute," the nurse said, "let me get someone."

She rushed out of the room and came back a minute later with a doctor.

"So, Mr. Armstrong," the doctor said, "you decided to join us again."

Walter pointed to the tube.

"Okay, just let me run a few quick tests, and I'll pull that out of there."

The doctor examined Walter, taking his temperature, blood pressure, and listening to his heart and lungs with his stethoscope.

"Everything seems to be in order," the doctor said, "so the tube's coming out. But you'll still be with us for a while. It's going to take you a few weeks to recuperate. We'll have to run some more tests to rule out any permanent damage. Hypothermia is very serious. You're a lucky young man. That sleeping bag probably saved your life."

I didn't want to see them pull the tube out, so I ran to the nurses' desk and had the nurse call home for me.

Mamie answered the phone.

"Hi," I said. "Uh... can I talk to Dad?"

"He's not here," she blurted.

"I wanted to tell him that Walter's awake."

"Somebody already called. He's on his way."

When I went back to Walter's room, he was alone. The head of his bed was raised so that he was half sitting up... without the tube in his mouth. He flashed a weak grin at me.

"Hey, you!" he said, his voice really low and raspy.

I sat down on the bed beside him, pulling the heavy electric blanket up to his neck. I was concerned because a nurse had told me that he was still having shivers off and on, and he had some tingling in his toes, which might be a sign of frostbite.

"Do you remember anything?" I asked.

"I remember seeing a really bright light," he said. "I was drawn to it. It was such a peaceful and spiritual experience. But then I heard *your* voice calling me away from the light. When I turned to see what you wanted, the light was gone. Now you see what you've done? You talked me right out of heaven!"

6

What Friends Are For

Dad picked Walter up from the hospital a few days later. Of course, we were all excited that he was coming home. But none of us knew how Mamie would respond to Walter, because she hadn't seen him in a week. After her ugly encounter with Pat at the hospital, she was too embarrassed to go back there again.

Because Mamie didn't allow us to be in the living room, Joyce, Pat, and I kept finding excuses to go to the kitchen or the garage, so we could peek out through the living room window on the way by to see if the car were coming.

When it finally came, I opened the front door, not caring what Mamie would say. After all, since Walter was just getting back from the hospital, she couldn't expect him to come in the back way.

As Walter climbed out of the car, he looked a little weak. It was obvious that he had lost quite a bit of weight. But when he saw me, he got the biggest smile on his face.

Dad walked around to the passenger side to give him a hand, but of course Walter declined the help, supporting himself on the car until he got his balance. Then he started slowly walking toward the house. At the steps, he held on firmly to the rail to pull himself up. Once he made it to the front door, Joyce and Pat greeted him with warm hugs.

As he slowly walked through the living room toward the kitchen, he kept stopping to get his balance and catch his breath.

Joseph ran up and grabbed his hand to give him support.

Suddenly, from behind us, we heard Mamie's voice.

"Sit down," she said, pointing toward the couch.

We were all shocked by her gesture of friendliness.

As Walter sat down on the normally forbidden couch, Mamie took a seat in the armchair across from him.

The rest of us, including Dad, stood there taking all this in.

"Your sisters have been splitting your chores," Mamie said. "I guess that will go on for a while, because the doctor said you should just rest for a few weeks."

"I'm helping, too," Joseph piped in with a big smile.

Walter gave Joseph a wink and then turned back to Mamie.

Not one to waste words, she stood up to walk away, then turned around and paused for a moment.

"That was some stunt you pulled," she said. "You scared your sisters half to death."

When Mamie was back in her bedroom, Pat got down on her knees in front of Walter and said, "How can we serve you, Master?"

We all laughed. The next few weeks, Joyce, Pat, and I teased him about how we had to wait on him all the time.

By the beginning of December, when Walter had been home from the hospital for three weeks, Mamie was still being nice to him. Was it possible that she was actually human?

Life was starting to seem a little more bearable. I had made a new friend at school who attended the same church I did. Her name was Phyllis. I shared all my family secrets with her. Aside from Melissa, she was the only person I had ever done this with.

Phyllis persuaded me that it would be a good idea to talk to her older sister, Sandra, and her husband, Ernest. Sandra was Phyllis's legal guardian because their mother had died of cancer two years before.

Mamie allowed me to visit Phyllis on Saturdays and Sundays if I completed my chores. One Saturday, Phyllis, Sandra, and I went shopping. Sandra insisted on buying me an outfit for the Christmas play we were performing at our church. I was afraid of Mamie's reaction when she saw it.

When we got back to Phyllis's house, Sandra called Mamie and explained that she had taken us both shopping and bought me an outfit for the church play. Phyllis and I couldn't hear the response, but Sandra gave us the thumbs up. Both of us were jumping around, holding our mouths, when suddenly we heard Sandra ask Mamie if I could spend the night.

"Phyllis and I are going to the movies," she said, "and we'd like Reesa to join us. It'll be late when we get out, so she may as well sleep over. I'm so grateful that Phyllis has Reesa, because Phyllis has been so lonesome since our mother died."

Phyllis and I were just standing there glaring, with both fingers crossed.

"Okay, okay, I understand," Sandra said. "Thank you. Goodbye."

Sandra hung up the phone and turned to us.

"Yes!" she screamed.

Phyllis, Sandra, and I began jumping and yelling.

"I can't believe she said yes," I said. "We're *never* allowed to spend the night out. Only to Aunt Minnie's. You were great!"

Sandra smiled.

"I do have a B.A. in psychology," she bragged. "Just make her think she's doing you a favor."

That evening, after Ernest got home, we all went to the movies. Phyllis and I sat together and talked all through the movie. I told her about Melissa and Marshall and how we had agreed to meet every summer. Phyllis asked if she could come up with me next summer. I was sure it was okay, and promised her I would double-check with Aunt Minnie.

Then we directed our attention to Ernest and Sandra, who were sitting three rows in front of us. Every time they tried to kiss, we would throw popcorn at them. But that didn't stop them. We had so much fun that I almost forgot my real life. As Mamie popped into my mind, a blanket of sadness enveloped me. Phyllis saw my pain and made the silliest face. That did it! We both burst out laughing.

When tomorrow comes, I thought, *I'll have to go back to reality. But today I'm free, and I'll live for this moment.*

After the movies, we went out for burgers and shakes. When we got back to the house, Ernest and Sandra sat me down in the living room, and Sandra said, "Let's talk."

I began shifting my weight back and forth in my chair, glaring straight ahead, avoiding eye contact with them. I was good at that. I perfected the stare as a shield to protect myself against all those people who pretended to care about me. People like Mamie's friends or relatives, or some of the ladies at church.

Phyllis walked over to me, and stood directly in front of my face.

"I promise we'll help you," she said, "and *she* will never know."

I began to blurt out my secret twisted life, going on and on for I don't know how long, until suddenly I heard sobs. Looking up, I saw Sandra was crying, and Ernest was pacing around with a glass of water. Then there was a crashing sound. I looked toward Ernest, and saw that he had slammed the glass up against the wall.

"I knew it! Damn it, I could tell they were being abused. All the signs were there. The same fear, and the shame that I experienced growing up with my abusive stepfather."

"He suspected all along," Phyllis said. "He saw through the façade. He said abused children learn how to survive. They learn to protect their abuser and never answer questions directly. The more invisible you are, the better."

That night, I was adopted by a new family. Ernest vowed to help me any way he could. We all knew that Mamie had the law on her side. Sandra and Ernest were not family and couldn't get us out of the house. But there were ways to make life more bearable.

I slept so peacefully that night, and again I had a levitating dream. This time, I was floating above Walter, Joyce, and Pat, trying to tell them that they could levitate, too. But they couldn't hear me. When I woke up, I wasn't sure for a moment whether I had actually been levitating, or if it was all a dream.

On Sunday morning, when we arrived at church, Mamie was waiting for us, with Joseph hanging on to the back of her skirt, as he usually did. Sandra gave Mamie a big hug and told her how much it helped Phyllis to have me over. Mamie was all smiles, thinking she had done a good deed.

I was overjoyed, thinking about my weekend, and couldn't wait to tell my siblings. But the Pastor was especially long-winded that day, and the service went on for three hours.

Once church was over, we all congregated in the back, and my brother and sisters flooded me with questions. "Did you go to the movies?"

"What did you see?"

"Why did she let you sleep over?"

"Wait, wait!" I responded, and slowly began to tell them about my weekend, trying not to leave out a single detail. I wanted them to feel as if they had lived the experience with me. When I told them about the conversation with Ernest and Sandra, I could see the alarm on their faces. But I told them that Ernest had been abused as a child and recognized the signs we exhibited.

"They'll help us," I said. "We need *someone* to help. We can't go on like this."

Phyllis and Ernest walked up, and Phyllis said, "Let's go."

We all looked puzzled.

Ernest motioned toward the entrance of the church, leaned in close to us, and whispered with a smile, "I've cleared it with the drill sergeant!"

We all ran out the door.

"Sandra's gonna take your stepmother shopping while we have some fun," Ernest said.

"How did you pull *that* off?" Walter asked.

Signaling for us to get into the car, Ernest replied, "It was all Sandra's idea. She knew Mamie couldn't pass up going shopping for Christmas."

We went to a restaurant around the corner from the church, and were all enjoying our meals, except for Walter, who seemed preoccupied. He kept looking at the busboys and asking Ernest questions about them.

Finally, Ernest said, "Would you like to work here?"

"Mamie would never let me. Besides, I couldn't even get here... it's too far."

"If I can work it out, would you like to be a busboy here?"

Walter's face was beaming as he shook his head up and down. "Yes, yes!" came bursting out of his mouth.

After finishing our meal, we went back to the church.

"Okay," Ernest said, looking a little apologetic, "we're gonna dust all the pews and empty all the trash cans. That's one of the bargains I made with Mamie so you could come with me."

Pat immediately replied, "It's a pleasure just not to be in her presence!"

"That's Mamie alright," I whispered to Pat. "She always likes to have things clean."

"Yeah," Pat said in a loud voice, "so long as *she* doesn't have to do any of the work."

After we all finished cleaning up, we had an hour to chat before the evening service began at 6:00 p.m. While we were sitting around, Sister Johnson came in, and said to Walter, "Oh, how clean the church is! I know you guys did it. Sister Armstrong has done such a great job with you children."

Walter gave her a casual "thank you" as Joyce and I forced smiles.

But Pat rolled her eyes and said, under her breath, just loud enough for me to hear, "Why don't you ever get *your* brats to clean the church?"

After the service, Sandra and Phyllis took Mamie and Joseph home. Ernest drove my siblings and me home; first, he stopped at one of the local liquor stores to get us some ice cream.

When we pulled up to the house, we were all a little startled to see Ernest get out of the car and head for the front door. We didn't know what to do. He was an adult visitor, but we were not allowed to enter the house through the front door. This created a very awkward and embarrassing moment for us all.

Pat, of course, was the one to break the silence. "The servants enter through the back," she said with a smirk. "It's a custom since way before slavery, I hear."

Ernest looked terribly sad.

Giving him a gentle shove toward the front door, Walter said with a smile, "It's okay. Rome wasn't built in a day."

By the time the rest of us ran around to the back, cleaned off our shoes, and put on our house slippers, Ernest was already sitting in the living room, talking with Mamie. From what we gathered, listening from the next room, the manager of the restaurant in Elizabeth City was a friend of Ernest's and had asked for his help in finding some young men to work there. Ernest assured Mamie that it wouldn't be a burden to get Walter back and forth to his job because his church was right around the corner from the restaurant where Walter would be working.

"It would be a great opportunity for Walter," he emphasized. "Working helps to build character, and the manager and I will both be looking out for him."

Mamie was hesitant, and Ernest had to repeatedly assure her that everything would be fine. Finally, she agreed.

Walter began to weep softly like a little child.

"What's wrong?" I whispered, not understanding his reaction.

After a few moments of silence, he said to me, "Over the years, I've built a shell around myself for protection. I never expect anything positive."

He and I were as opposite as night and day. Faith is what I depended on for my absolute survival. Without it, I was convinced that I would surely die. Walter, on the other hand, always anticipated the worst. Mamie's agreeing to allow him to work took him completely by surprise. That's why he lost control of his emotions.

Looking at the rest of us with complete sincerity, he said, as if making a vow, "I will save up all my money and get us out of here. We will all leave together, I *promise!*"

I believed Walter.

The following weekend Walter started working at the restaurant.

After church that Sunday, Ernest asked Mamie if he could take my sisters and me to lunch with Sandra and Phyllis at the restaurant, and she said he could. When we got there, we were so proud to see Walter working. He was so happy.

To our surprise, as we were reading the menus, Dad, Mamie, and Joseph walked in.

Ernest hurriedly got us a bigger table, and we all moved to it. But the atmosphere had turned chilly, and all conversation stopped.

Trying to lighten the mood, Dad said, "So what are we eating in this joint? Fancy hot dogs on a popsicle stick, or what?"

"Dad," Joyce said, "you know very well those are not popsicle sticks."

The manager appeared at the table and introduced himself to Dad and Mamie. "Hi, you must be Walter's parents," he said. "It's a real pleasure to meet you. I'd like to compliment you on raising such a hard-working son. In the brief period he's been here, Walter has impressed everyone."

As he was talking, I could see that he couldn't take his eyes off Joyce. At one point, it was so obvious that he forgot what he was saying right in the middle of his sentence.

Ernest jumped in to rescue him. "Where are my manners? This is Spence, everyone."

And then Ernest walked around the table and introduced each of us by name. When he got to Joyce, he put his hands on her shoulder and said, "This is Joyce. . . the one you were admiring so much, you lost your train of thought!"

Spence turned five shades of red. "I couldn't help it," he said, "she's so beautiful!"

Joyce put her head down, blushing. I was amazed to see my older sister being wooed by a man. Apparently, the smile that was plastered on my face was embarrassing to someone, because I suddenly felt a kick to my leg. I looked across at Pat, who was rolling her eyes and squeezing her lips tightly together, to signal that I should wipe the smile off my face.

At that point, the cashier beckoned to Spence. "Sorry," he said, "I have to get back to work. Enjoy your meal. . . it's on the house!"

As Spence walked away, he glanced back, winking at Joyce.

Sandra drove Joyce, Pat, and me home. We had to drag Joseph along; he was whining and crying because he didn't want to stay for the evening service.

When Walter got home a little later, we were waiting for him.

As soon as he walked in the door, he taunted Joyce, "Guess what Spence said about you?"

"What did he say?"

"He likes you, and he's gonna ask Dad if he can be your boyfriend."

Pat blurted out, "What makes him think she *wants* him for a boyfriend? He has to ask *her* first."

Looking at Joyce, she said, "Don't be so gullible. Play a little hard to get."

Joyce was just staring into space. You could see she was already smitten.

That night I could hardly sleep, thinking about Joyce and Spence as girlfriend and boyfriend. I imagined her getting out of Mamie's house and living happily ever after!

As the weeks went by, Walter would come home and give Mamie his paycheck, which made her very happy. She kept telling him she was saving it for his future, but we all knew better. However, Spence and Ernest had worked it out so that Walter got *two* checks—one for his hourly pay, and the other for overtime. Ernest and Sandra had taken Walter to a bank and opened a savings account for him. Ernest would deposit Walter's overtime checks for him and let him see his account anytime he wanted to. Walter also got tips in cash from the waitress at the end of the shift. Mamie wasn't aware of any of this, so he put his money in a coffee can, dug a hole under the house, and placed a large rock on top of it. Walter let all of us dip into that can whenever we wanted, although there weren't too many opportunities for us to spend money. Nevertheless, it was a newfound freedom, and Walter was so proud to help us.

By this time, Dad had been out to sea again for a while, so we were all looking forward to his return. Life wasn't much better when he was around, but at least we ate a little better, and Mamie had to produce some type of excuse for the beatings and punishments she dished out.

Joyce had been seeing Spence for about six weeks now, without Mamie being aware that they were dating. Sandra would create reasons or chores for Joyce to come to her house, and Spence would meet her there.

There were a few close calls, though. Once Mamie called Sandra's house and wanted to talk to Joyce when she wasn't there. We were all on pins and needles, knowing that she was on a date with Spence. I felt scared.

This will ruin everything! I thought. *She'll surely find out.*

But Sandra was brilliant.

"Oh, I sent her and Phyllis to the laundromat," she said, "to do some heavy laundry that my machine couldn't handle. I'll go and pick Joyce up early if you like."

But Mamie was satisfied. "Just tell her to call home when she gets back," she said.

After that, Joyce and Sandra set up a system. Joyce would call in every hour unless there was no phone where she was. But most of the time, Joyce and Spence would simply try to stay close to a phone. If Mamie called, Sandra would make up some excuse and have Joyce call home right away.

7

Submission

A few days after Dad got home, he and Mamie went out for the evening. We waited our allotted time to make sure they were not returning. But just as Walter and I were about to dart over to Phyllis's house through the back door, we saw Pat motioning us back.

Dad and Mamie were just pulling back into the driveway at the front of the house.

What a close call!

Then we remembered that Joyce was on the phone in the bathroom, talking with Spence.

Walter ran for the back door, hoping to knock on the bathroom window, signaling Joyce to get off the phone. However, it was too late. Mamie was standing outside the bathroom door, listening to the entire conversation. Pat had run outside and began tapping at the window to get Joyce's attention. Then she pointed toward the door and made a face. Joyce walked out in her bathrobe, head down, phone in her hand. She was trembling.

Mamie snatched the phone from her and began swinging the receiver across Joyce's face. Putting her hands up, Joyce attempted to block the blows.

Dad appeared out of nowhere. "What's going on?" he asked.

Mamie was wild. Spit was coming from her mouth as she started calling Joyce names. "You loose little tramp! You're gonna get pregnant, and every bone in your body will open, and if it doesn't close right, you'll be crippled for life!"

Dad stepped in between them, and Mamie immediately retreated to her bedroom.

Joyce was weeping. "I was just talking to a boy from school," she cried.

Mamie came back as wild as ever.

"Strip!" she yelled, and began hitting Joyce with the extension cord.

Joyce started to move toward her bedroom, but Mamie grabbed her arm and demanded, "Strip right here!"

Joyce looked at her with disbelief.

"Not in front of Dad and Walter," she murmured.

Mamie tore Joyce's robe off, exposing her nakedness. Dad turned away and went to his bedroom, but Walter just stood there.

As Mamie began to tear into Joyce's skin with the extension cord, Walter walked in front of Joyce, facing Mamie. She swung the cord several times, striking him across the face and chest. I could see his body twitch with each blow. I'm not sure whether it was more from pain or anger. But other than the twitching, he showed no emotion.

As I stood watching this, Walter was a superhero in my eyes. And for the first time, I saw a glimpse of fear on Mamie's face.

Later that evening, I asked Joyce why she had said she was talking to a boy from school.

"If she finds out it was Spence," she said, "she'll never let me see him again, and it could also jeopardize Walter's job."

Little did we know that Walter's job was already at risk. Mamie has started creating her vicious plans against Walter. We should have been prepared for her to retaliate because Walter had now stood up to her twice

The next morning, as Walter got dressed for work, Mamie walked into his room and said, matter-of-factly, "Don't bother! You no longer have a job!"

Tears began to roll down his face, and a horrific groan came from his belly, as if he were being whipped with the extension cord.

"Besides," Mamie said, "you haven't been helping your brother do his homework since you got that job. That's why he's failing in school now. Get in that dining room and sit at that table and help him with his homework, now."

Walter bit his lip and clenched his fists. But then, thinking better of it, he spun around and walked into the dining room, where Joseph was working on his homework. As Walter sat down, he grabbed one of Joseph's books, flipped it open, and then slammed it down hard on the table.

"Why can't you *get* this stuff?" he said. "I've gone over this with you a million times."

Joseph started crying.

This brought Mamie out of her bedroom. She stood over the two of them, glowering down at Walter.

"He can't seem to remember anything," Walter said. "Or maybe he just doesn't want to. You should think about having him checked out."

Joseph stood up, leaned in close to Walter, and said, "I hate you!" and spat in his face.

Walter just sat there for a moment. Then he looked up at Mamie, expecting her to do something. Instead, she just turned and walked away with a smirk on her face.

I was convinced that she was a demon from hell with a mission to destroy us all.

Joseph ran to his bedroom, crying.

Walter got up from the table and calmly went to the bathroom to wash his face. When he came out, he picked up the phone in the kitchen, called Spence, and said he would be in to work. Then he put some clothes in a pillow case.

There was so much sadness in his voice as he said to us, "I can't stay here anymore. I'm sorry. I wanted us all to leave together. I'll come back and get you. Leave the cash can under the house. When I can, I'll leave you money there."

I was crying, but I knew he had to go. "Where will you stay?" I asked. "Don't sleep outside. Promise me you won't sleep outside!"

"I promise," he said. "Now I have to go." He opened his arms wide, and each of us gave him a hug. Then he walked right out the front door.

An hour later, Mamie came out of her bedroom. "Where's your brother?" she asked, looking around as if he were hiding behind us.

Pat was more than glad to tell her. "He left," she shouted. "Packed his clothes, and he's never coming back!"

"Oh, he'll be back alright," Mamie shrieked. "I'll just call the police. He better not go to that job." Her smirk was gone now, and there was a trace of concern in her voice.

I decided to join in. "Well," I said, "he used the phone before he left. I heard him say something about going to live with Mother."

She rushed past me with a shove that knocked me to the floor.

Pat helped me up, muttering, "Maybe you *do* have a backbone."

Mamie was on the phone in her bedroom, telling Dad that his son was lazy and useless, and insisting that he call the police and have them pick Walter up.

We couldn't hear what Dad said, but we didn't think he would call the police.

Two days later, Phyllis came over and told me that Walter was staying with a friend whose parents were sympathetic. Spence had agreed to let him work in the back, just in case Mamie or any of her relatives dropped in. Of course, that meant that Walter would lose his tip money, but he didn't care.

For the next several weeks, we got constant updates about Walter from Phyllis and Sandra. When we talked about this, we had to make sure that Joseph wasn't lurking around, because he would surely tell Mamie everything.

Dad would say, "I'm sure you all know where he is, because Reesa would be bawling her eyes out by now if anything were wrong."

Aunt Minnie also figured out that we knew where Walter was, since she would call and say, "Now, I don't want to know too much, but just that he's safe." And we would reassure her that he was fine.

One day, Mamie answered the phone in her bedroom, and it quickly became apparent to Joyce, Pat, and I that it was Aunt Minnie, and she was letting Mamie have it. I whispered to my sisters to go into the kitchen. Phyllis had taught me how to pick up a phone without making it click, so I did that, placing my hand over the mouthpiece, and the three of us listened in.

Aunt Minnie was just saying, "If you weren't so mean to them, he wouldn't have had to run away. The last time, he almost died. Wasn't that enough for you?"

"I'm not mean to them," Mamie said defensively. "They're defiant. You don't live in this house with them. They sneak around and do dirty little things behind my back."

"Because you forced them to! They don't act like that when they're here with me."

Mamie apparently had no answer for that, just before slamming down the phone, she let out a deep breath and said, "I'll tell Joseph to call you when he gets home."

The three of us enjoyed having a little power for once. But that didn't last long. That Friday evening after school, Mamie said to us, "One of you better tell me where your brother is before you *all* get in trouble!"

We wouldn't budge, so she decided to punish us by not letting us eat a single thing for the entire weekend. By Saturday night, my stomach was aching so badly that I cried myself to sleep.

On Sunday morning, when we woke up, Mamie had Joyce cook bacon and eggs for her and Joseph, and then ordered Pat and me into the dining room to watch. As he ate his food, Joseph kept looking at me with a grin.

If she leaves him alone, I thought, *I'm gonna slap that smirk off his face!*

After church, Phyllis tried to talk to me, but Mamie was watching our every move, and Joseph was standing nearby. It seemed pretty clear that Mamie had turned him into a spy, so Phyllis and I could only make small talk.

That evening, Joyce grilled a steak and baked potatoes for Mamie and Joseph, with a salad on the side. The two of them sat there like royalty, slowly eating their dinner. When they were done, Mamie called Pat and I into the dining room and ordered us to clean up.

I took the plates into the kitchen, and just as I was about to throw the scraps away, Joyce stopped me. "There's still steak left on the bone," she whispered. Then she took a bite and offered some to Pat and me. Standing over the trash can, with tears running down our cheeks, we shared the scraps from Mamie's plate.

On Monday morning when I arrived at school, Phyllis was waiting for me. With great embarrassment, I told her about how Mamie was not allowing us to eat, and how we had devoured her leftovers the night before. She gave me a hug and offered me her lunch bag.

Shaking my head, I said, "I can't take your lunch."

"Sure, you can," she replied. "I'll go to the office and call Sandra. She'll bring us both lunch."

"Thank you," I sighed.

That evening, Dad said to Joyce, "I'm craving spaghetti. I took the ground beef out of the freezer this morning."

When Joyce went to the kitchen sink to get the beef, she saw that Dad had taken out enough for all of us. So we finally got to eat a real meal.

When Walter had been gone about two months, Phyllis came running to our house, out of breath. She didn't come over often without Mamie's permission, but when something was important; she would sneak into the garage and wait for an opportunity to signal one of us to come out. This time, it was me who saw her.

"We think the police got Walter!" she exclaimed. "He was going to work at night, and the neighbors said he was stopped by the police!"

Hearing voices, Joyce and Pat came out to the garage. Phyllis's news made all of us frantic.

"You better go, Phyllis," I said. "Mamie will be home any minute."

We spent that whole day on pins and needles.

That evening, as we were preparing for dinner, I went out to the garage to set the table. Suddenly, there was a noise behind the curtain that divided the garage in two. Before I had time to respond, Walter came out with a huge grin on his face.

"What happened?" I whispered with relief. "Phyllis said the police picked you up."

"Yeah," he said softly with a smile, "but my friend's parents told them about my living situation here, and they let me go."

"Why did they stop you anyway?"

"Curfew, Minors can't be out alone past ten o'clock."

"So, what are you gonna do?"

"I haven't got that far yet. It's not a good idea to stay at my friend's house anymore, just in case the police have a change of heart. Ernest said I could stay with him and Sandra a while, but I don't want to impose. I would have to sleep in Phyllis's room or the living room. That's too much to ask."

An idea popped into my head.

"Just stay here!" I said. "They'll never know. We eat in the garage, so we can just put extra food on our plates, and during the day you can stay at Ernest and Sandra's. You know they won't mind. Phyllis said Ernest was going crazy trying to find you after he heard the police picked you up. Go and tell them, and I'll leave the garage door open."

Walter was shaking his head. "You're really crazy!" he said. "If she catches us, you know what will happen."

"Who cares? What's one more beating?" I was shocked by my own words.

Sneaking back into the house, I motioned for Joyce and Pat to follow me. But Joseph was there and followed them, so Pat got a cookie from his jar, poured out half a glass of milk, and led him to the dining room table. That would buy us at least ten minutes. Before heading into the garage, Pat grabbed two more cookies for us and closed the cookie jar very quietly so that Mamie wouldn't hear it from her bedroom.

When Pat joined Joyce and me in the garage, I told them that Walter had been hiding here when I came out to set the table.

"Where's he now?" Pat asked, looking behind the curtain.

"He went down to Phyllis's house until it's safe," I said. "We can't take a chance on him sleeping outside again, but he can sleep here at night. They'll never know."

"We could put his sleeping bag out here in a box," Pat said.

"Wait here," Joyce said, and left the garage for a moment. When she came back, she said, "We can't leave the door to the kitchen unlocked. She checks it all the time, especially since Walter's been gone." Then, with a big smile, she dangled some keys over her head. "Remember when she lost her keys? Well, I found them and never told her!"

She pulled a roll of masking tape out of the high cupboard and ripped off a piece. Sticking it on the outside of the kitchen door, near the top, she said, "This will be our signal that she's asleep. When Walter comes into the garage and wants to get into the house, he can find the key here, but he must always put it back on top of the cupboard every time so it won't get lost."

"You know what?" I said. "Walter could sleep under my bed. That'll be much warmer than the garage, and she'll never find him there."

Joyce looked at Pat.

"What do you want?" Pat asked suspiciously.

"We have to tell Walter about the key and the tape… and going to Reesa's room. Can you distract Mamie so I can get to the phone and call Sandra?"

"Oh, no!" Pat grumbled. "Let Reesa do it. She's a better suck-up than I am. The witch will see right through me. You know I can't be in her presence very long without blowing it."

They both looked at me.

"Okay, I'll do it," I said. "But you two owe me *big time*."

That night, I heard Walter creep into my room. "I'm gonna sleep in the garage," he whispered. "She may get up and hear me if I'm in here."

Putting my hand over his mouth, I pulled him to the closet. Mamie didn't allow us to keep anything on the closet floor, so normally it was bare. I only owned two pairs of shoes, one for Sunday and one for weekdays, and they were usually on a shelf, along with a sleeping bag for cold nights. But now I had the sleeping bag on the floor, as well as a pillow from my bed.

"Look," I whispered, "all the comforts of home in your miniature bedroom. And for once you get to close the bedroom door!"

He chuckled.

"Fancy that!"

We kept Walter hidden that way for over six weeks.

Then it was time for Dad to go out to sea for another one of his three-month tours of duty. He was concerned about Walter, although he was pretty sure we knew where he was.

Mamie pretended to be concerned, too, but mostly she was just embarrassed that one of her little soldiers had gone AWOL. Everyone at the church was asking her about Walter, and she had to lie that he had gone to visit relatives. By now that story was getting old.

We had constructed a plan, which Spence now put into action.

He called Dad and told him that Walter had been in contact with him about his job and would be meeting him on Friday.

We waited nervously until Friday arrived. Dad never said a word about this to any of us before he left home that day without Mamie. The plan was that Walter would only surface if Dad showed up alone.

Countless hours later, around nine that night, as I lay in my bed, totally awake, I heard Dad come in.

A moment later, he said softly, "Walter, wash up and go to bed."

As Walter passed my open door on the way to his room, I didn't know whether to be jubilant that he was back out in the open or terrified that Mamie would kill him.

Mamie's unrelenting screaming all night long kept the entire house awake. She was ranting like a madwoman, "I don't want him here! He has disrespected me! How dare you go behind my back?"

We kept trying to hear what Dad was saying, but he was whispering.

The next morning was quite interesting because Mamie stormed into Walter's room and began telling him how selfish he was by putting his family through all the worry and humiliation. Then she told him that he had to return to work at the restaurant and pay the family back for six months, on top of losing all the money she had already put away for him.

Of course, Joyce, Pat, and I, who were listening to all this through the walls, knew that she had long ago spent that money on herself.

Walter just replied, "Yes, mama, I'm sorry."

When Mamie left the room, we all ran in there and looked at Walter with amazement, dumbfounded by his humility. But after he filled us in on his agreement with Dad, we all understood. He had told Dad that he would only come back on one condition, which was that he gets to keep his job. He didn't care about the money Mamie kept, because he knew she was spending it anyway. Dad didn't want to leave home and hear that Walter was sleeping outside somewhere or in trouble with the police. Appealing to Walter's loyalty to us, he expressed his concern over being away so long with no man in the house. Walter wanted Dad to understand that his sacrifice was neither for Mamie nor for him. He never told Dad that he had been staying in the house for the past six weeks. Instead, he led him to believe that he had spent the entire time with friends who had given him food and shelter.

8

Reality Check

When Dad left for sea, all was quiet. But Mamie had a taste for blood, and we could tell she was just waiting for one of us to slip up. One evening, as we were all getting ready for bed, I suddenly heard my name bouncing off the walls. I ran to Mamie's bedroom and found her lying on her bed.

"Yes, ma'am?" I said as I entered.

"Have you had your monthly?" Her little black beady eyes were staring at me.

"Yes, ma'am," I lied, "I'm on my monthly right now."

She sat up on the side of the bed and said, "So when were you gonna show me?"

Stuttering no louder than a whisper, I said, "Uh...tonight."

"Don't go to bed without showing me," she ordered, and motioned me out of the room as if I were a little puppy.

Joyce and Pat snatched me in the hallway.

"What are you gonna do now," Joyce asked, "Since your period stopped two days ago? Didn't I tell you to show her?"

"I forgot, I forgot," I said, as tears streamed down my face.

I gave Pat a look of desperation, hoping she was on her menstrual cycle.

She snapped at me, "You have to grow up, Reesa! There's no time to forget. She's gonna beat the hell outa you!" She turned away as tears welled up in her eyes.

Just then, I saw a pair of big brown eyes peering around the corner of the hallway. It was Joseph, spying on us. "What are *you* looking at?" I snapped, taking my anger out on him. "Get away from here!"

Joseph darted into his room and closed the door.

Walter came out of the bathroom with his hand to his forehead, deep in thought. Suddenly he snapped his fingers.

"Where are the pads?" he asked.

Joyce pointed to the cabinet under the sink, and he reached in and got one.

I looked at Pat, knowing that this was taking from her stash.

"Sorry," I said, "I'll get one from Phyllis."

We were only allowed to change pads twice a day, and each of us had fourteen pads per month.

Walter said, "Reesa, what's on your foot?"

As I bent my head down to see what he was talking about, he swatted me in the nose. Everyone gasped! Then blood started streaming down my face because my nose bled very easily. I instinctively put my hand to face, but Walter pulled it away and stuck the pad under my nose.

With red eyes, I whispered, "Thank you!"

"Anytime," he said with a smile.

Once again, he was my superhero.

During the following weeks, Spence was at our house quite often. He had a way of charming Mamie. On the weekends, he would pick her and Walter up and take them to Elizabeth City, an hour drive away, dropping Mamie off at her sister's and Walter off at the restaurant. Then he would come back to our house and spend the day with us or take Joyce out somewhere. It was really easy to plan our day then, because neither Mamie nor her sister could drive. Mamie assumed that Spence was at work with Walter. In the evening, Spence would pick Walter up at the restaurant and then get Mamie.

One Saturday, it was Joyce's birthday. While she and Spence were out, I called Phyllis and told her I wanted to bake a surprise cake for Joyce—her favorite kind was chocolate with white icing. Phyllis brought over colored sprinkles and candles from her house. When we were just finishing up, Pat came home from shopping. She had bought Joyce earrings which we all knew Joyce had been dreaming about for more than two months. As Pat opened the package, my mouth dropped open.

"Wow! Where did you get the money for those?"

With my mouth wide open, Pat stuck her finger in it and said chuckling, "Close your mouth before a fly goes in." "Walter gave it to me, and it's a gift from all of us."

Phyllis pointed to the cake we had just finished baking.

Obviously impressed, Pat tilted her head a little, and asked, "You guys made this?"

She picked the cake up, carried it to the dining room table, and then went out to the front yard. When she came back, she placed white gardenias all around the cake.

"Now it looks like it came from a bakery," she said with pride.

At that moment, we heard Spence's car pull up, so Pat hurriedly lit seventeen candles.

As Joyce walked into the house, the three of us were standing in front of the table, smiling. Then we stepped away, revealing the cake.

Joyce just stood there enthralled

Finally, Pat said, "Blow out the candles before the whole house goes up in flames!"

Joyce blew out the candles and then turned to us with a big smile.

Pat held out a small box, and said, "Take it. It's from all of us. Walter wanted to be here, but he couldn't."

Joyce unwrapped the gift slowly, savoring the moment. This was the first birthday party we had ever made ourselves. The moment she saw the earrings, she began to cry.

Spence walked over to her and put his arms around her.

Pat smiled, and said sarcastically, "Don't cry now. Wait till you taste that cake. It looks good, but *those two* made it." She began to laugh.

We all sat down at the table with Mamie's best china. I made everyone hot tea, and the cake was delicious.

Spence suddenly jumped up.

"I better go," he said. "It's gonna take me an hour to get there. Can I have a piece of cake to go?"

He winked; Phyllis and I smiled with pride.

When Spence left, Joyce said, "Now it's time to work. We've gotta clean and dry every dish we used. Pat, you take the table area, and when you're done with that, come in the kitchen." Then she looked at Phyllis and me with such a serious face. "I need you two to remember *every* ingredient it took to make that cake."

Phyllis jumped up from her chair.

"That's easy," she said, running over to her purse and pulling out a piece of paper. "We used my mom's special recipe."

Joyce looked relieved. As Phyllis called out the ingredients, Joyce pulled them out of the cabinets and set them down on the counter. Phyllis and I were both puzzled by this at first, but it soon became crystal clear what Joyce was doing. Mamie would mark the food containers when she left for the day, so Joyce simply put marks a little lower, and Mamie would be none the wiser.

"What about the eggs?" I asked. "How can we replace the eggs?"

Joyce went to the refrigerator and pulled out the carton of eggs.

"You used three," she said.

Phyllis and I looked at each other, stunned.

"How did you know that?" I asked.

She showed us two dots inside the carton.

"Those dots indicate that two eggs were already used, and then there are three empty spots with no dots."

She took a pen and made dots where our eggs were missing.

Phyllis and I began to go through the cabinets to look at all the marks that were on the food. To our surprise, everything was marked. All this time, I had thought that Mamie had special powers or an incredible memory, but it was just little tricks.

I looked at Phyllis and said, "I wonder how many other tricks she's conjured up to catch us."

Phyllis got a peculiar look on her face.

"We have to think like spies," she said. "We need to get all the codes and never let her know we have the answers."

"That's great!" I said, "We're smarter than she is, after all. She can't even read and write."

After we marked everything and finished cleaning up, Joyce gave the rest of the cake to Phyllis to take home for Sandra and Ernest.

"We can't leave it here," she said. "Mamie has a nose like a bloodhound, and she'll smell that cake a mile away. You better hurry and go before she comes."

"Okay," Phyllis said, running out the front door. "But we'll save some for you when you come over."

Once Phyllis was safely out of sight, we closed the front door and opened all the back windows. Joyce wanted to be sure there was no aroma from the cake lingering in the house.

Then I got an idea. Running outside, I plucked a handful of gardenias from a bush, brought them inside, and placed them in a clear bowl of water, as I had seen Aunt Minnie do. Within minutes the entire house smelled of gardenias.

"That was brilliant!" Joyce said, heaving a sigh of relief.

When Spence finally brought Mamie, Joseph, and Walter home, he invited himself.

Mamie walked in and immediately screamed, "Reesa!"

I came running.

"Yes, ma'am?"

"Did you do that"? She motioned toward the flowers.

"Yes, mama," I stuttered. "I had no money for Joyce's birthday, so I gave her flowers from the yard."

She walked away mumbling something, came back with a bag, and handed it to Joyce, saying, "It's a little something from your dad and me."

Joyce opened the bag and pulled out a black sweater with a tag from the secondhand store still on it.

Joyce smiled, took a deep breath, and walked over to her.

"Thank you, mama," she said, "it's lovely."

Pat muttered just above her breath, "One of those token gifts. Give it back."

"What did you say?" Mamie said, turning on Pat.

"I agree with Pat," Walter jumped in. "What a thoughtful gift."

Pat looked both surprised and disappointed, since she was ready for a fight. But this time, for Joyce's sake, she didn't make a scene. Instead, she just turned her back to Mamie and walked away, rolling her eyes.

Spence walked over to Mamie and gave her a kiss on the cheek.

"I better go," he said, "it's getting late."

Spence waved to Walter to walk him to the door.

Mamie got up to retire for the night, but first spewed out some orders to everyone. "Clean this mess!" she began, referring to the bag the sweater had been in. "And Walter, make sure you lock the door after Spence."

"Yes, mama," Walter replied. Then he walked her to her bedroom door and closed it behind her, all to buy a few seconds for Joyce and Spence.

When Walter got to the front door, Joyce and Spence were engaged in a long passionate kiss.

"Enough already!" Walter said, breaking them up. "Go before she catches you two."

When Spence left, Walter locked the door and cleared his throat to get Joyce's attention as she was walking down the hall. He pointed to the crack of light under Mamie's door, to remind Joyce that Mamie was probably counting the footsteps that went by. Joyce tiptoed past Mamie's room on the other side of the hall, so Mamie wouldn't hear her. Then, as Walter passed Mamie's room, the witch hollered, "Did you lock the door?"

"Yes, ma'am," Walter responded, pointing to Joyce in an I-told-you-so manner.

That was one of the tricks we had discovered long before. Mamie would get down on her knees and look under the door to see which of us was going down the hall.

After that day, we perfected the game of getting Mamie out of the house so that Spence and Joyce can began to date on a regular basis.

I spent a lot of time with Phyllis, which didn't seem to bother Mamie. She was apparently preoccupied with something.

9

Deception

One day, when Mamie was at her sister's, Joyce ran into the house from her date with Spence. She was gasping for air and trying to talk at the same time. Leaning her head against the door, she slowed her breathing just enough to whisper, "I saw her... at a restaurant! Oh, you should have seen her!"

"Who?" Pat asked.

"*Who* did you see?" I asked, jumping up and down.

Walter ran to the kitchen and came back with a glass of water for Joyce.

Pat was her usual agitated self. Finally, she went up to Joyce and walked her to the sofa in the living room.

"Now, slowly," she said. "Who did you see at a restaurant? Is there anything we need to know?"

Joyce was holding her chest.

"It was Mamie!" she whispered.

We gasped.

"Did she see you?"

"No. She was with a man, and she was *kissing* him!"

"What?!!" Pat said.

I don't know who said what after that. The thought of Mamie kissing a man was more than I could imagine. Walter and Pat began drilling Joyce, wanting to know all the details. I was still suspended in time, trying to imagine a man in a restaurant being romantic with Mamie. I had never seen her display the slightest bit of affection for anyone other than Joseph.

I was snapped back to reality when Phyllis ran in through the front door, with Sandra and Ernest behind her. Phyllis began asking me questions about what Mamie was up to, but I didn't know what to say.

Then Joyce said to all of us, "Spence and I were having dinner at a restaurant outside Elizabeth City. We were in a quiet, dimly lit booth facing the entrance, when, all of a sudden, a couple walked in, laughing and talking. The lady was wearing a fake mink coat just like Mamie's. If it hadn't been for that coat, I wouldn't have paid her any attention. Anyway, she was being very nice and loving to the gentleman she was with. As the hostess greeted them, I saw the woman's face and was shocked to realize it was Mamie!"

Spence jumped in, "I was looking at Joyce's face when she turned as gray as a ghost. I stood up to see what she was looking at, and what I saw, made me unable to move. I was just stuck there. If Joyce hadn't snatched my coat to pull me down, Mamie would have seen me."

We were all screaming with a mixture of curiosity and disbelief.

Walter piped in, "So, what else happened?"

Joyce began pacing back and forth.

"You'll never believe who the guy is." Before we could guess, she blurted out, "Her so-called cousin George."

Pat jumped straight up. "I told you that Mr. George wasn't her cousin. Didn't I tell you? He was always coming over here when Dad was gone. How about those times we came home from school, and he was here? Mamie was walking around in her bathrobe like she was sick. How disgusting! She was in Dad's bed with him!"

As Sandra and Ernest looked on in disbelief, Walter said, "I never liked the way he was always looking at Pat's and Joyce's behinds."

"Yeah," Pat said. "And one day, he made a pass at me. I was so disgusted; I threatened to tell Dad. He was afraid after that and never tried it again."

Pat was sitting on the edge of her seat, rocking back and forth.

"So now that we know," she said, "what are we gonna do about it?"

I began swinging my arms as if I were in a classroom being asked a question by the teacher.

"I'm telling Dad," I said, "and he's gonna leave her!"

Pat walked over and put her hand over my mouth.

"You will do no such thing! And he would never leave her anyway."

Sandra took control of the conversation.

"Pat's right," she said. "You cannot under *any* circumstances tell your dad. How will you explain that someone saw her in a restaurant? I'm sure she'll deny it, and it couldn't possibly make your life any better."

Walter was pacing around. "It's really a good thing," he said. "We can use it for our benefit. Think about it. This is why she's been so preoccupied recently." He paused for a moment as he tapped his fingers on his forehead. "But we need some tangible evidence, like a picture of them together."

"Don't worry," Spence said, "I can get the picture. I'll just introduce myself to the manager of the restaurant and tell him some story about this couple. I just need to know how often they go to his restaurant."

Suddenly, a thought occurred to me.

"Do you think Joseph knows?" I blurted out.

"He's just a kid," Pat said. "How would he know about adultery?"

"But where is he when Mamie is with Mr. George?" I asked.

"That's why she takes him to Aunt Bea's all the time," Pat said.

I was so angry. I made up my mind that someday I would tell Dad everything. Mamie had committed the ultimate betrayal in my eyes, and I wanted her exposed.

It ended up taking Spence a while before he could get the pictures of Mamie and George together. We were expecting Dad home in less than a week, and I had almost given up hope that Spence would get the shot.

I started being very friendly with Joseph, hoping to get some information out of him. I gave him candy and helped him with his artwork. He loved to draw. I figured, since Mamie didn't drive, that Mr. George would pick her up at her sister's house, and Joseph would see him.

"So, what did you do at Aunt Bea's yesterday?" I asked. "Did you go to the park with mama?"

It was painful for me to call Mamie "mama," but I was playing a necessary role.

"No, I just played," he said sadly.

"Did mama have to go somewhere with Mr. George?"

"Yeah, they had to take care of some kind of business again."

Yeah, business! Right!

One night, about three weeks later, when Mamie was at her sister's, Joyce was waiting for Spence to show up to take her to the movies. As soon as his car pulled up, she ran outside.

Phyllis and I were in a world of our own, trying on lipstick that Phyllis had brought over.

Joyce came back in the front door and dropped an envelope in my lap.

"I'll be back in two hours," she hollered on her way out the door.

I opened the envelope and pulled out three pictures of Mamie and her lover.

My emotions went from disgust and contempt to outright rage.

How dare she pretend to all those church people that she's so holy and sanctimonious!

My mind began to race back to all those days she would make us repent in front of the entire church if we were caught lying or doing something she considered ungodly. Somehow I would expose her. Looking over at Phyllis, I could see that she was reading my mind.

"We have to make sure," she said, "that Mamie doesn't suspect you all in any way."

I nodded.

That night, we all agreed not to show Dad the pictures or to tell him about the affair until we could be sure of the consequences. Walter hid the pictures in his money can under the house.

A few days later, Dad's ship was scheduled to come in. Spence told Mamie that he would take her to meet the ship, and asked if we could all come. For some reason, she agreed.

Dad would only be home for a little over a week, and then he would be sailing out for eight more weeks. Our meeting him at the ship would be a rare occasion for him. Usually, he would have to catch a ride home with one of his shipmates.

As I watched the ship pull up to the dock, I was trying to figure out a way to expose Mamie without the others getting angry at me. It occurred to me that maybe I could get Joseph to spill the beans without realizing it. I figured I would have to talk to Joseph when I knew Dad would overhear us, but no one else would be around. Then I could slip in something about Mr. George. The thought of it made me feel good.

The ride home, with eight of us in Dad's car, was cramped. I had to sit in the front seat between Dad and Mamie with Joseph on my lap. Spence and Joyce were so packed next to each other in the back seat that you could barely tell they were two separate people. Dad kept looking in his rearview mirror to keep an eye on them.

Spence invited us all to dinner at the restaurant, and Mamie and Dad agreed.

Usually, at dinner, we would each take turns saying grace. This time I volunteered.

"Please bow your heads," I said. "Father, thank you for the food we are about to receive, and bless the hands that prepare it in your name, amen."

Everyone paused. Mamie looked up and said, "Scripture!"

We each had to memorize a passage of scripture for after grace. I usually just said, "Jesus wept." This time I was waiting for her, because I knew she would try to embarrass me the first chance she got. I cleared my voice and said, "Thou shalt not covet thy neighbor's wife."

I heard a choking sound and looked up to see that it was Mamie. Dad had to get her a glass of water. Still coughing, she got up and went to the restroom. Dad followed her to the door.

All of us but Joseph were laughing so hard that I thought I would wet my pants. When Dad and Mamie returned to the table, Dad looked baffled.

"Where did you get that scripture from?" he asked.

"From the Bible," I replied. "It's one of the Ten Commandments that I'm studying. You know exact instructions from God on what you're not supposed to do." That was a phrase Mamie used all the time.

But on this night, she didn't say another word. It was one of the quietest evenings with her I can remember.

Later, when I was preparing for bed, Joyce and Pat sneaked into my room, and Pat whispered, "We know what you're up to."

"You can't do it," Joyce said. "You cannot expose her right now. When the time is right, we'll tell him."

"Okay," I said, reluctantly giving up my plot.

The next day, at school, I told Phyllis what had happened at the restaurant. She laughed so hard. But then she suddenly stopped and looked at me suspiciously. "You don't intend to *tell* your dad, do you?"

Shaking my head, I said, "I won't tell him now, but one day he'll know the kind of woman he is married to."

Just then, Linda Adams, one of the most popular girls in school, walked by with her group, and I stopped talking in mid-sentence. Linda's clothes were always the latest styles, and she wore her hair straight with just a little curl on the end. That year, 1966, white was popular, and she had on the shortest white skirt I had ever seen. On top, she was wearing a baby blue sweater that buttoned down the front. Some boys were hanging around her like groupies.

Once Linda's group had passed, Phyllis snapped her fingers in front of my face. "Oh! Where was I? Did you see those skirts? And only two of them had on socks. Linda was wearing pantyhose. Her parents must have a lot of money. She always dresses so nice and never wears socks."

Phyllis stood up.

"Come on," she said. "Let's get a head start before the bell rings. Sandra says those girls are fast. She had a friend like that who now has two babies and no husband."

The warning bell rang, so we had to hurry to our biology class. As we ran, I looked at Phyllis. "I don't want to *be* like them," I said, "I just want their *clothes!*"

Phyllis laughed. "You're crazy," she said, smiling.

Yeah, just a little.

Biology was one of two classes that Phyllis and I had together.

I felt so much more confident when I was in a class with her, even though, in biology, we sat on opposite sides of the room. On this day, however, our teacher had us in groups for our finals, so Phyllis and I were in the same group, along with two other girls and one boy.

Alfonzo Taylor always tried to get into our group because he knew he could goof off. He called us the "brains." We did all the work, and he would do the presentation. He loved showing off by speaking in front of the class. The girls in our group were shy and gladly allowed him the chance to be in the limelight.

I was so excited that school was almost over. Just one more day after this, and we would be out of school for the whole summer. Phyllis had finally told me in a letter who her secret crush had been all year long. I wasn't at all surprised because I had seen her sneaking peeks at him more than once. I told her my secret crush in my own letter. This was an end-of-the-year ritual.

As I was passing my letter to Phyllis, it dropped on the floor just as Linda Adams was walking by. She picked it up and began to read my note out loud. The teacher was out of the room for a minute, so Linda had free rein. Embarrassed, I just put my head down. There were lots of whispers and giggling in the room.

Then, without warning, Alfonso Taylor was standing over my desk. He dropped the torn letter in front of me.

"I would *never* go out with *you*! Sure, you're a brain, but that's all!"

I was so humiliated that I just stared straight ahead throughout the entire session. When class was over, I was the first to leave. But Phyllis caught up with me.

"Hey, don't cry over him. He's not worth it."

Tears were streaming down my face. "I'm not crying over him," I said, choking on my tears. "He made himself feel good at my expense. He's way too shallow. I'm sure he'll get his payback someday."

The next day was our last day of school. I just wanted the day to be over with. In fact, I wanted the whole week over with. We were going to Aunt Minnie's on the weekend, and since Sandra had agreed to let Phyllis stay with us the whole time, this promised to be my best summer ever. So my two best friends, Phyllis and Melissa, would get to meet, and we would all spend more than two months together. Mamie, of course, wasn't aware of this arrangement.

In my homeroom class that morning, we had to hand in all our books. As I sat at my desk, waiting for the teacher to call my name, I was a little fidgety because I could feel a lot of eyes looking at me. So I just sat there staring at my hands. When I heard my name, I jumped up to hand in my books and get my promotion slip to eighth grade. But Alfonso was standing in front of my desk blocking my way. He was shifting his weight back and forth.

"I uh—" he started to say, as I heard my name called again.

Looking him straight in the eye, I said, "It's okay. I hope your looks will get you an A next year."

He put his head down, and I walked past him on my way to the teacher to get my slip. As I left the room to go home, I had a big smile on my face.

Phyllis popped out of her homeroom class, and we both screamed, "Let the summer begin!"

10
The Plot

I hurried straight home so Mamie wouldn't have any excuse to keep me from going to Aunt Minnie's for the summer. As I turned the last corner, I saw a police car in front of the house, and Mamie was standing at the front door talking to a police officer.

I ran around to the back, and as I entered the house, I saw Joyce putting some peroxide on Pat's face.

"What happened?" I asked.

Walking over to Pat, I gasped as I saw that she had a bloody bruise on her forehead, and her lip was swollen and bleeding. Tears were rolling down her face, and she was shaking.

"I *hate* her!" Pat exploded.

Joyce quickly put her hand over Pat's mouth, but Pat snatched it away.

"I don't care! I *hate* her, and I wish she was *dead*!"

The front door of the house suddenly slammed, and Mamie darted into the kitchen out of breath. She grabbed Pat by the arm and dragged her to Pat's bedroom. Sweat was beading up on her forehead as she ordered Pat to strip.

Pat reluctantly took off her clothes, covering her face to keep the blood from dripping onto the floor.

Mamie left the room and came back with an old bed sheet that she began tearing into strips.

"Lay face down on that bed!" she commanded.

When Pat did, Mamie tied her hands and feet to the four bedposts with the strips and started slapping and punching Pat, who lay there without making a sound.

Joyce and I were watching this scene from the hallway, when

Mamie suddenly turned around and ordered me to "go get the cord!"

We all knew that she kept it on the inside knob of her bedroom door, but I just stood there frozen. For every tear that Pat was holding back, I was shedding a hundred. In fact, I was crying so hard that I could barely breathe.

Mamie stomped past me, knocking me into the wall. When she came back with the cord, she began hitting Pat so hard that welts immediately rose up on her body. Then Pat started twitching involuntarily, and screamed so loud that the walls literally shook.

Finally exhausting herself, Mamie dropped the cord on the floor and stormed out of the room.

Joyce ran in and untied Pat's arms and legs. We were all crying. Pat just lay there, broken. Joyce covered her body with a sheet. We were so preoccupied with Pat that we didn't know what Mamie was up to. She came back into the room, shoved me off the bed, snatched the sheet off Pat, pulled her up onto her feet, and pushed her to the bathroom.

When I ran to the bathroom door, I saw that Mamie had filled the tub with steaming hot water.

"Get in!" she ordered Pat.

Trembling, Pat slowly stepped into the tub. As she tried to sit, Mamie pushed her down into the scalding water.

Pat screamed out in pain.

"You stay there till I tell you to move!" Mamie shouted, and then dashed out of the bathroom and slammed her bedroom door behind her.

Pat huddled in a corner of the tub, pulling her knees up to her chest.

Joyce motioned for me to follow her to the garage.

"Let's just turn on some cold water," I pleaded.

"No, she'll hear that. I have a better idea."

Joyce went to the freezer and grabbed two bags of ice. She tore them open and poured the cubes onto a towel.

"Go first and make sure she's not coming," she whispered. "And be quiet!"

I ran ahead, and then came back to wave Joyce on.

When Joyce quietly slipped the ice cubes into the water, I could see instant relief on Pat's face. She even tried to smile.

I stood there bewildered, shaking my head.

Suddenly, I heard a noise behind me, and turned to see Joseph staring in horror at Pat.

"Shh," I whispered, putting my finger over my mouth, and led him to the kitchen. Handing him a cookie, I said, "Now, be quiet. Don't say anything about this."

He shook his head with tears in his eyes. Pat was his favorite. As he ate the cookie, I knew he wouldn't tell on us.

After an hour, Mamie came out of her room and told Pat to get out of the tub and go to bed.

"Now you two can kiss her wounds. And by the way, she just ruined your summer."

On the way out, she banged the bedroom door behind her.

As we cleaned Pat up, she kept apologizing. Finally, she was able to tell us what had made Mamie so furious.

For our Physical Education classes, we were supposed to wear shorts, but Mamie didn't want us to show off our bodies, so she insisted that we wear dresses over our shorts. Joyce and I went along with that nonsense, but Pat refused. She would show up for P.E., but sit out the class without any explanation. Therefore, the P.E. teacher had given her a D on her report card.

Pat changed the grade before Mamie saw the report card, and that would have worked if the teacher hadn't called to make sure that Pat didn't have a hidden health problem or anything else she should know about.

Mamie went to the school and showed the teacher the report card. Then she slapped Pat across her face right in front of the entire class. Of course, Pat didn't take that too well, and ran away. But the truant officer found her a few blocks from school, and when she refused to go back to class, he called the police. Mamie showed up and hit Pat right in front of the police officer. She hit her so hard that Pat slipped and fell, banging her head on the curb. The policeman told Pat how blessed she was to have a parent who cared about her, and warned her that he would put her in juvenile hall if she tried to run away again.

I waited until I was alone that night to grieve about the summer I had looked forward to for so long. I cried quietly into my pillow.

About two o'clock in the morning, Pat and Walter came into my bedroom and woke me up. My eyes were so swollen from crying that I could barely see them. As I yawned, I asked them, "What's going on?"

Focusing, I could tell that something serious was happening. There was a chill in the room. They were frightening me even though neither of them had said a word. Then Joyce appeared, but she didn't speak, either.

Finally, Pat started to say something. I could hear sounds, but I couldn't make out the words. I felt as if I were looking down at them from the ceiling. We were all there, and I could even see my body, but my spirit wasn't there.

Suddenly, I could understand what Pat was saying.

"Basically, there's no other choice. I'm gonna kill her."

Walter interrupted her. "No, *we're* gonna kill her."

I looked at Joyce, who was always the voice of reason. Her silence spoke volumes.

Then she said, "We'll discuss the details tomorrow. Just go to sleep."

They all walked out and went back to their beds.

I don't know how many times I dozed off that night. I kept thinking I was having a dream, but it was so vivid.

When I jumped out of bed the next morning, I ran to Joyce's room. She avoided my eyes.

So it's real! It wasn't a dream.

All day long, I kept saying to myself, "Mamie is going to die!"

There was so much tension in the house. Pat's loathing for Mamie had permeated every room.

Early that evening, after Mamie went out shopping with a friend, we waited for Walter to come home from work. When Ernest pulled into the driveway, Phyllis jumped out of the car with Walter.

"Give me a minute," she said to Ernest.

When she came in, she was all cheery and ready to make plans for the summer. Not wanting to tell her our scheme, I said, "This is not a good time to talk. Come back in an hour. I'm sorry."

She looked confused as she said, "Alright, I'll come back later."

When Ernest drove away, we all sat down on the living room floor, since that was more comfortable than Mamie's plastic-covered couches.

"Once the act is done," Walter said, "there'll be no turning back."

"I don't want you guys getting into trouble," Pat said. "I can do this all by myself."

We all shook our heads.

"No," Joyce said. "We're all in this together."

"No one else is to know about this," Walter said. Then, looking at me, he added, "Not your best friend," and he turned to Joyce, "not your boyfriend. No one."

"How are we gonna do it?" Joyce asked.

"Poison!" Pat said.

"It can't just be any kind," Walter said. "Let me check with my friend who works at the hospital. We have to be smart about this."

"Maybe, but we need to move fast," Pat said.

I started to realize that this was actually going to happen, and that terrified me.

"Are you sure we really want to do this?" I asked.

Pat turned to me with a decisive look on her face.

"I can't spend the whole summer here with her, day in and day out," she said. "It's impossible for me to hide my hostility. I'm so angry I can't even sleep at night. I lie awake trying not to go into her room and kill the bitch!"

As she spoke, Pat gently touched her lips, which had swollen so much that they were twice their normal size.

"Don't worry," I said. "They'll heal. I guess I better call Phyllis and tell her not to come back."

Lying in bed that night, I felt so violated, so raped of my innocence.

Why did I have to come here?

I mourned for my past, for the little girl I used to be. I mourned because even now, as impossible and painful as my life was, I was going to an even darker place.

I may never laugh again.

Pat had visible and tangible scars as proof of her pain. In my case, I had no literal scars, but my heart was aching. It was as if an invisible knife were sticking in me, twisting and turning back and forth. Wanting to cry out, I put the pillow over my face and bit down on it. I screamed and screamed until I passed out from sheer exhaustion.

When I woke up the next morning, my body was weak, and I could barely pull myself out of bed.

In the hallway, Joyce saw me and knew right away that something was wrong with me.

"Clean yourself up, you look a mess," she said. "Did you cry all night?"

I nodded.

She grabbed a towel, wet it with cold water, and started wiping my face.

"You've got to pull yourself together, Reesa."

I couldn't speak. I just stood there, shaking my head.

Dad came home that afternoon. He would be staying a few days before shipping out for the summer. By this time, he had become an ordained minister in our church, and was spending more time there than before. There were revival meetings all week that he and Mamie went to, so we had more peace than usual from her—except when we had to teach her to memorize scripture so she could pretend to be reading when she had to read aloud in church.

One day, Dad, Mamie, and Joseph left the house early because Aunt Bea was sick, and Mamie wanted to visit her before going to church.

The moment they were gone, I called Phyllis. In what seemed like seconds, she was coming through our front door. I was so obviously upset that she started trying to pry things out of me. But I was careful not to tell her about our plot to do away with Mamie, since we had all taken a vow of silence.

Phyllis was openly disappointed about our aborted plans for the summer, but tried to be optimistic.

"Maybe she'll change her mind. Or how about your Aunt Minnie? Do you think *she* can help?"

I thought about what would happen if Mamie told Aunt Minnie we couldn't come.

"Hey, you're right!" I said. "I don't think Mamie's told Aunt Minnie. Dad would have said something by now, or Aunt Minnie would have blown her stack."

I bounced up to find Joyce, with Phyllis right on my heels. Joyce listened to our reasoning and agreed to call Aunt Minnie.

"We'll have to call collect," Joyce said, "so it doesn't show up on the bill. I'll do the talking. I don't want you to slip up. Wait here while I go call."

Phyllis looked at me with a puzzled expression.

"Slip up *how?*" she whispered in my ear.

I just shrugged my shoulders, pretending not to know that Joyce was referring to our plot.

When Joyce came back, she looked confused.

"You're right," she said. "Aunt Minnie had no idea. And she said if Mamie tries to keep us from coming, she's gonna raise hell!"

I couldn't wait to tell Pat that now there was a glimpse of hope and possibly we would be getting away from Mamie for the summer, after all. At the moment, Pat was off shopping with Sandra, who was trying to pick up her spirits.

With Mamie out of the house, I invited Phyllis to watch some TV with me.

Walter came home from work at dusk. When he saw Phyllis and me in front of the TV set, he said, "What are you doing?" and quickly closed the curtains. "I could see the TV a block away. And where are the towels?"

I went and got two towels from the garage, ran cold water in the kitchen sink, and dumped them in. Dropping my head, I said, "I'm sorry, I forgot. I'll look out."

Phyllis followed me as I turned the lights off in Walter's room and sat down at his window. She sat there scratching her head, and finally asked, "Can you tell me what this is all about?"

Looking at her, I realized that she was as naïve as I was when I first arrived from Boston. This crazy life had become so routine that I sometimes forgot what it was like being normal.

"We're not allowed to watch TV," I explained. "During the day, it's pretty easy to get away with it. But at night, if the curtains are open, she can see the light from the TV when she turns the corner, so we close all the curtains."

"But what are the wet towels for?" Phyllis asked.

"Good question!" I smiled. "The first thing Mamie does when she comes in the house is feel the TV to see if it's hot. So we take turns looking out. The moment we see the car, we turn off the TV and put cold towels over the set to cool it down."

Phyllis looked so sad that I gave her a hug.

"It's not so bad," I lied. "We read a lot."

Walter walked in. "I'll take over so you two can go and watch TV," he said.

On Friday morning, it was time for Dad to leave. Everyone began to cry as he packed his duffel bag. He tried to joke a little to keep me from crying, but that was out of my control.

When the military car came to get him, I was in the bathroom, throwing up.

Knocking on the door, he said, "Reesa, I'm leaving."

When I came out, I grabbed him by the neck and didn't want to let go.

Feel my innocence! I screamed inside my head. *See me now, because the next time you see me, my innocence will have died!*

He had to peel my arms away.

During that day, while Walter was at work, Aunt Bea's daughter arrived and took Joseph away to Elizabeth City for a few days.

"It's time for spring cleaning!" Mamie announced.

She had Pat and Joyce washing and ironing for hours, and I had to fold the sheets and pillowcases after they ironed them. Everything in the house had to be washed, ironed, and folded just right. Besides that, the drapes had to be vacuumed. Also, all the baseboards and windowsills had to be scrubbed.

Around 8:30 p.m. that night, as usual, Mamie ordered us to take our baths and get ready for bed. I was the last to take my bath. When I walked into the kitchen, Joyce and Pat were having a difference of opinion that was starting to get too loud.

"I can hear you all the way down the hall," I said, stopping in my tracks when I saw what Pat was up to.

In her hand, she was holding a bottle of rat poison that Dad kept locked in the outside shed.

I gulped. "I thought we were supposed to wait for Walter."

Joyce grabbed the bottle.

"We are!" she said.

Pat was stirring a cup of hot tea.

"She's going to sleep now, so we don't have time to wait for Walter," Pat said.

Just as she walked out of the kitchen with the cup, we heard Walter come in the back door.

Looking around and seeing the expression on our faces, he said, "Where's Pat?" But he didn't wait for an answer. "We have to stop her!" he said, looking frantic.

Joyce ran to Mamie's bedroom door and knocked.

"Mama," she called, "can I come in?"

She opened the door quickly and saw Pat standing there, handing Mamie the cup of tea. Joyce rushed past Pat and bumped into Mamie, knocking over the tea. Then she started jumping around.

"I think I have some glass in my eye!" she cried. "I dropped a glass, and it feels like there's splinters in my eye."

Mamie was so irritated that Joyce had spilled her tea that she simply started fanning both of them out of her room.

"Look at the mess you've made! Get this up and get out of my room! Pat, help your sister!"

Pat was so angry that she literally dragged Joyce to the kitchen.

"What in hell was *that* all about?" she yelled.

Walter grabbed Pat by the arm. "Calm down," he said. "I told her to stop you. First of all, you agreed to wait for me." He was shaking his head in disbelief. "Dammit!" he said, slamming his hand on the counter.

Everyone was silent.

"Spence said he's supposed to pick us up tomorrow and take us to Aunt Minnie's house. She's just not telling us, and she told him not to tell me. Don't you see, she's just being hateful?" He turned and looked at Pat. "And by the way, that junk you used will just make her sick. I was getting something more powerful from a friend at the hospital. You're not ready to do this. You can't just do it off the top of your head."

We washed the cup, saucer, and spoon, to get rid of the evidence, and put away the rat poison.

"Walter, are you sure about Aunt Minnie?" I asked.

"Yeah! I called her just to make sure she's still expecting us."

Joyce turned off the kitchen lights, and immediately turned them back on.

"*That's* why she's had us cleaning and ironing all day," she said, "so she'll have nothing to do while were gone."

I went to bed that night and slept soundly for a change. It didn't matter about working all day like little slaves. I didn't care about Mamie deceiving us or her hatefulness. I only knew when I woke up the next morning; I could be *me*—nothing more, nothing less, just me!

11

Undercurrent

I was awakened abruptly the following morning by Mamie roaming through the house like an invading army. She snatched my covers off, yelling, "Get up and start packing!"

I turned to look at the clock. It was 5:30 a.m. in the morning.

"You have one hour to get your things packed and be ready to go," she shouted.

Then I heard her thumping down the hall, going from room to room.

At 6:30 a.m., everyone was packed and dressed, sitting in the living room waiting for instructions.

The moment Mamie appeared in the room, a cloud of friction hovered over her and Pat. But Pat somehow managed to control herself. She just stared straight ahead with a tight jaw.

Mamie looked at Pat the whole time as she spewed out instructions and insults. Finally, still not taking her eyes off Pat, she stood up and said, "Your ride is here. Enjoy your summer."

We all rushed out to the car, throwing our bags in and never looking back.

As we took off, Spence appeared to be even more eager than we were. There was so much chitchat in the car that we almost missed seeing Mr. George.

But then Pat hollered out, "Wait, look!"

Just before we got to the expressway, Mr. George was coming down the exit ramp.

"Turn around!" I said to Spence. He looked at Joyce, who nodded in agreement, so we made a quick U-turn.

"Go down the side street," Walter said. "You can see our house from there, but she won't be able to see us."

At first, we didn't see Mr. George's car. But as Spence pulled up, there it was on the side street.

"He's at the door," I yelled, pointing just in time to see Mamie standing in her bathrobe letting him in. It was all crystal clear now why she had wakened us up at 5:30 a.m. and practically shoved us out the door.

Unwilling to allow her this deception one more minute, I lunged out of the car and darted for the back door. My adrenaline had me racing so fast that Walter couldn't catch me, although he tried. I hit the back door with so much force that it shook the whole house. Mamie didn't have time to think. She was openly startled as she stood at the kitchen stove.

"Did something happen?" she said, trying to sound concerned.

"I forgot something," I said as I walked through the house.

Mr. George came out of Mamie's bedroom, tucking his shirt in his pants.

Mamie tightened the belt of her robe.

"Oh!" she said. "This is Mr. George. Do you remember?"

Cutting her off, I said, "I know who he is."

Then I walked to my room and grabbed my book bag.

The two of them were huddled in a corner, but stopped talking when I came back. I walked toward the back door and then stopped in my tracks. Testing the moment, I walked to the front door. Then I turned, looked at her, and stared at the two coffee cups on the table and his shoes beside the sofa.

"You two have a nice summer," I said dryly, closing the front door behind me. I walked out to the driveway and stood there until Spence drove up. As I climbed into the back seat, the mood was somber. No one said a word as we drove away.

Finally, Walter cleared his throat, and asked, "Are you gonna tell us, or what?"

Spence pulled the car over, and he and Joyce shifted in their seats to face me. I poured out all the details of what had happened in the house. We all sat there captivated by the enormity of what had been revealed and its possible consequences.

Mamie was having an affair, and now she knew that we knew. The whole thing seemed to excite Pat, who turned to me and said,

"She's on notice now, but be aware of the undercurrent when she regroups."

The others nodded in agreement.

"I really don't care," I said. And at that moment I didn't.

"Well, at least now we know why she got rid of Joseph," Pat said.

I couldn't wait to get to Aunt Minnie and tell her the news. When I saw her, I blurted out all the sordid details, hardly pausing to take a breath as everything came pouring from me as though this would be my only chance to tell her. She sat listening without interrupting me, and when I was done, she got up and hugged each one of us.

"That's a lot to absorb," she said, "but we have all summer."

We all felt relieved.

Aunt Minnie walked over to Spence, gave him a big hug, and said, "So *you* must be Spence." Turning to Joyce, she said with her familiar little giggle, "You have your auntie's taste!"

Then she herded us into the kitchen, where, as always, she had prepared a feast for us. When I saw it, I took a deep breath to appreciate the blend of aromas. The kitchen was literally swimming with eggs, bacon, sausage, and homemade biscuits, with fresh fruit and flowers adorning the counters and windowsills.

As we were eating at the large round kitchen table, a sudden squeak of the screen door got everyone's attention, and then, Melissa came in.

I jumped up to hug her, and we were screaming and jumping around until Walter got up to give her his chair.

"Where's Marshall?" he asked, heading for the door.

"Right across the road, at Granny's," Melissa said. "We didn't recognize the car, so I volunteered to come over and see if you all had made it."

With that, Walter was out the door.

After helping Aunt Minnie clean up our breakfast mess, Melissa and I sat out on the back porch for hours, swapping stories.

Finally, Melissa said, "Come on, Marshall wants to see you." As she said this, she was blushing.

I grabbed her hand and ran upstairs with her, where I slipped out of the long dress I had on and into some tight jeans and a T-shirt.

Melissa rolled her eyes at me with a big smile.

"I got these from Phyllis," I said. "Wait till you see my other outfits when she gets here in two days. I couldn't bring them because Mamie was checking everything."

Taking the braids out of my hair, which Mamie made me wear all the time, I let my hair down and brushed it into a ponytail. Then I lightly patted on some lip gloss, pressed my lips together, and took a last look in the mirror.

"Okay," I said, "let's go!"

As we ran across the road, I could see Walter on the porch. He was facing us as he talked to some guy who had his back to us. I knew it wasn't Marshall because he was much taller and more powerfully built. As we approached, I kept wondering who it could be.

When we got to the porch, the guy turned around, and his face lit up when he saw me. Then he grabbed me and kissed me right on the lips! Our embrace must have gone on a little too long, because Walter cleared his throat in a way that clearly meant "Break it up!"

As we pulled apart, Melissa was covering her face with her hand to hide her smile.

"I wanna show you something," she said, taking my hand and gently pulling me into the house.

When we were out of earshot, I gave her a shove and said, "Why didn't you tell me that Marshall had gotten so tall and handsome? I hardly recognized him."

She shrugged. "Whatever. He looks okay." She tilted her head down and looked up at me. "What was that kiss about? Maybe we need to talk some more. Did you leave something out?"

"It's gonna be a *gooood* summer!" I said with a big smile.

We both giggled, and then ran to find Walter and Marshall.

For the next two days, as Melissa and I waited for Phyllis, everyone would sit on the front porch for hours talking to Aunt Minnie and playing games. Spence was at the house all the time. Aunt Minnie loved him, and he obviously had a lot of respect for her.

We all noticed that Aunt Minnie seemed to be slowing down

quite a bit. For one thing, she let Joyce and Spence do all the grocery shopping, which she never would have done before.

On our second evening there, while Melissa and I were playing checkers, Walter and Marshall came running over. I noticed that Marshall was holding his right hand behind his back. Then he put out his hand in front of me, holding a small fruit jar that was pulsating with light.

"You remembered!" I said, beaming.

"Of course! Didn't you say that lightning bugs were one of the things you miss most about this place?"

I was really touched, because this was the very first gift I had ever been given by a guy.

"Enough already!" Melissa said. "Let's not get mushy"

"Let's go to the movies," Walter said.

"There's a new one starting tonight," Marshall added.

I looked over at Aunt Minnie.

"Go ahead," she said. "I'm fine. It's a little late for me anyway."

I hopped up and kissed her on the cheek.

"Thank you," I whispered in her ear.

At the sidewalk, I asked, "Hey, how are we gonna get there?"

Marshall pointed to the car in his grandmother's driveway.

"I've had a driver's license for six months," he said, giving me a little wink.

Melissa and I got in the back seat, while Walter and Marshall got in front. When we arrived at the theater, Melissa and I sat together, with Walter to my left, and Marshall to his left. When the coming attractions began, Walter and Marshall left to get popcorn and drinks, and when they returned, Marshall sat down beside me, and Walter sat on the end.

Melissa and I were talking throughout the movie, but I couldn't help noticing the butterflies in my stomach every time Marshall touched me. About halfway through the movie, I felt his arm slide around my shoulders. Then he leaned over and whispered, "I really missed you."

Looking up at him, I smiled and said, "Ditto!"

When the movie was over and we were all walking to the car, Marshall took my hand. A little self-consciously, I glanced over at Walter and Melissa, but they hadn't noticed anything because they were busy talking and laughing about something. I knew they thought of each other as brother and sister. Besides, Walter had a girlfriend in town that he had met at the restaurant.

Noticing my obvious distraction, Marshall stopped and turned me to face him. Looking humble as his eyes searched mine, he said, "I was serious about you being my girl last summer, and I've talked to Walter. He's okay with it."

I was trembling, but managed to smile.

He walked me to the car, but this time he opened the front door on the passenger side, and I slid in. Walter and Melissa got into the back seat. So it was now official: Marshall and I was a couple.

The next day, Melissa and I spent all morning and afternoon doing each other's hair and playing with makeup. Phyllis would be arriving in the morning, so our excitement was mounting.

While we were in the middle of this, Marshall came running into the house so hyper that we could barely understand what he was saying.

"Slow down!" Melissa snapped.

"Sorry," he said, trying to compose himself. "Walter just called. Some guy at the restaurant quit, and Spence agreed to give me the job. But I've gotta go and get some white shirts and a black tie. Come on!" he said, swinging me around. "Go to the store with me."

As we started out the door, I turned to look at Melissa, who was standing there with a sad look on her face. Marshall went over to her, picked her up, and swung her over his shoulder. Then he carried her out to the car, where, after opening the door for me, he dropped her in the back seat like a sack of potatoes.

"You'll always be my girl," he said with a big smile.

As Melissa straightened her blouse, she fussed at him, "Sometimes you act like a big kid." But I knew she was happy that we were including her. I made a mental note to be more sensitive in the future and make sure she didn't feel like a third wheel.

The next morning, Spence dropped Phyllis off right on time, and she and Melissa clicked right away, as I knew they would.

While the three of us were chatting away, Pat came down the stairs all made up.

"Oooooh!" I said. "Look at *you!*"

"Where are *you* going with *that* on?" Melissa said.

Phyllis laughed.

Pat just brushed us off.

"You Three Stooges just mind your business!" she said with a smile. Then to Aunt Minnie, who was sitting out on the back porch, she shouted, "I'll be home early tonight," and strolled out the front door.

Phyllis was stunned at the difference in Pat. As she watched her walk out, she said in a soft voice, "She's beautiful!" Then, turning to me, she broke into a huge smile and said, "Speaking of beautiful, wait till you see what Sandra sent you."

As we carried Phyllis's bags upstairs, she kept taunting me.

"Let's see now, what bag is it in?" And she gestured back and forth, from one bag to the other.

When we got to my room, I opened the bag I was holding and found a white box wrapped with a blue satin ribbon and a bow on top. Phyllis walked over, picked up the box, and pushed me onto the bed, where Melissa was already sitting.

"Open it!" Phyllis ordered.

I gently slid the ribbon off the box, making sure not to mess up the perfectly tied bow. When I lifted off the lid, I burst into tears. There lay a soft blue sweater and a little white skirt. And I mean *little*.

"How did she know?" I said through my tears.

Phyllis was grinning. "It's your birthday present."

"But my birthday's in February."

"I know, but we wanted you to enjoy your gift and not worry about when you'd be able to wear it." Grabbing some tissues and handing them to me, she said, "Clean up and don't be so mushy. Most of the stuff in this bag are the clothes you had already hidden at my house, so now you get to unpack it."

We stayed up all night putting on makeup, doing each other's hair, reading our diaries to each other, and telling stories. When the sun came creeping through the windows, we realized that we hadn't slept a wink all night. Then, one by one, we started to crash.

12

Never Been Kissed

The next thing I knew, Joyce was shaking me.

"Get up!" she griped. "It's two o'clock in the afternoon! We had to listen to you guys laughing and talking all night!"

Our bodies were lying every which way on the double bed. Phyllis was stretched out with her head hanging off one side, Melissa was lying across the bottom, and I was curled up in a corner at the head.

As Joyce poked us, we slowly started rolling out of the bed. Sitting up and looking at each other, we couldn't help laughing.

Joyce came over, grabbed my chin in her hand, and turned my head side to side.

"Mamie's gonna *kill* you!" she hollered, so loud that Pat came rushing through the door to see what was wrong, with Aunt Minnie right behind her.

Pat took one look at me, and said, "Who *did* that?"

Melissa piped up, "*I* did. Do you want me to do *yours*?"

"Yes!" Pat answered

All this happened so fast that it took me a moment to realize what they were all talking about.

We rushed downstairs, where the bottle of rubbing alcohol was still on the kitchen table. Melissa took some cotton balls and rubbed alcohol on Pat's ears, while Phyllis pulled some ice out of the freezer. When she walked over to the table with the ice, Pat pulled away.

"What's *that* for?" she asked.

I looked at her reassuringly. "It's alright," I said. "The ice will freeze your earlobes, so you won't feel the needle at all."

While Phyllis was holding the ice to Pat's ears, Melissa told me to get the broom in the pantry and pull out a piece of straw. When

I did, she took a pair of scissors and cut the straw into two pieces. Then she set fire to both ends at the gas stove. Taking one of Pat's earlobes between her fingers, she pinched it hard, but Pat showed no emotion. Melissa looked at me and pointed to the needle that was soaking in the alcohol. Pat looked at me apprehensively. I walked over and put my hands over her eyes, and within seconds Melissa was done.

Pat jumped up and ran to the bathroom. A minute later, she came out with the biggest smile on her face that I had ever seen.

"Thank you!" she said to Melissa, hugging her. "Thank you so much!"

We tried to persuade Joyce to get hers done, too, but to no avail. She wouldn't budge.

I couldn't figure out if she was more afraid of Mamie or the pain.

After that, I didn't see Marshall for two days, because he was training at the restaurant. On Saturday morning, I got up early, wanting to catch him before he left for work. But I saw his car wasn't there.

Nevertheless, I knocked on the door and walked in. Just like at Aunt Minnie's house, the door was never locked, and we came and went as we wished.

Marshall's grandmother was sitting in the living room, drinking a cup of tea.

"Good morning, Miss Pearl," I said. "Did Marshall leave for work already?"

"Yes, baby, he had to leave early today."

"Have you had breakfast yet, Miss Pearl?"

She was quite old, and I knew she would often skip meals if no one paid attention.

"Melissa's making me something," she said.

Since Melissa was back at Aunt Minnie's house, I knew that wasn't true.

"I'll be back," I said, and went across the street to get her something to eat.

When I got back to the house, Phyllis and Melissa made endless efforts to cheer me up, but I was missing Marshall too much.

Finally, Aunt Minnie suggested that we go out and get our hair done. When we jumped at the idea, she called her hairdresser and told her we were coming. Before hanging up, she said, "Let that young girl Deborah do them. They'll like her."

Everyone in the salon knew Aunt Minnie. The owner said, "Your aunt was my first customer, over fifteen years ago." And then she introduced us to the other stylists as "Mrs. Minnie's girls."

A young woman came up in a red miniskirt, black boots, and big hair, wearing blue eye shadow that matched her blouse and white lipstick.

"Hi, I'm Deborah," she said. "Who's gonna be my first victim?"

Since Phyllis got her hair done every week, we decided that she should go first. She wore her hair short with long bangs, which always impressed me because most girls at that time thought they had to wear their hair long. She would get her hair relaxed—we called it "straightened" back then—and styled.

Phyllis showed Deborah a style she liked in a magazine, but Deborah took the magazine away from her and said, "That style's too old for you. I have something better in mind."

Phyllis was game.

Half an hour later, when Phyllis moved to the dryer, Melissa took her seat. She had long hair that naturally fell into beautiful curls, which I always liked, but she preferred her hair straight, so she had Deborah press it.

Finally, it was my turn. My hair, alas, was coarse and unruly and would not hold a press, so Deborah tried to talk me into getting it relaxed. Phyllis was all for it, since she had been doing that for years.

"I swear, it'll make your life a whole lot easier," Phyllis said.

Trusting her, I decided to go along with it.

"Well, then," Deborah said, "I've gotta go get some extra chemicals because, not only is your hair coarse, but it's virgin."

The woman sitting in the next chair said, "They better *all* be virgins!"

We all laughed.

When I got out of the chair, my hair was smooth and silky for the first time in my life, and I knew I would never press my hair again.

"We're too cute now," Phyllis said. "We can't just go home."

"Why don't we go to the movies?" Melissa said.

We all thought that would be great because there was only one theater in town, so it was a popular hangout for all the teens on summer vacation. We had great fun showing off our new do's to everyone.

It was getting dark when we came out of the show and a bit chilly, but none of us had brought a jacket. As we started walking home, shivering, I noticed a car flashing its lights. Melissa saw it, too, and began waving frantically.

"Come on, you guys, it's Marshall!"

As we ran to the car, Marshall jumped out to open the doors.

"Hey," he said, "Aunt Minnie was worried about the three of you. She said you left without jackets. I told her I could find ya'll." He winked at me.

When Marshall dropped us off at the house, he didn't hang around because he knew Aunt Minnie would be chewing us out. In fact, she was waiting for us on the front porch, and began scolding us for being out so long without calling home or taking jackets with us.

We all apologized and gave her a big group hug, which made her giggle.

"I promise I'll never worry you again," I said.

She squeezed my hand and wrinkled up her little nose.

"What are you gonna do about Marshall?" she said. "He was waiting here for you all day."

Phyllis and Melissa simultaneously said, "Go!"

Then Phyllis walked over to me and added, "I'm fine...we're fine...we'll be here when you get back."

"Thanks," I said with a smile.

As I ran across the road, I could see Marshall looking out the window. He opened the door just as I reached the porch.

"I'm sorry," I said. "I didn't know you were getting off early today. I came to see you this morning, but you were gone."

He looked at me apologetically.

"My grandma told me when I came home this afternoon. But let's not cry over spilled milk. I have something for you." He said these last words eagerly.

Then he led me to the overstuffed sofa in front of the fireplace, where he had a fire going.

Looking earnest as he handed me a small white box, he said, "I hope you like them."

I opened the box quickly. Inside, there was a pair of pierced earrings.

"How did you know?" I asked.

"Melissa told me," he said, and began to stroke my hair. His warm breath was close as he leaned over to kiss me.

I pulled away, avoiding his eyes.

"What's wrong?" he asked.

Nervously, I mumbled, "I don't want you to expect too much. I'm not. . . I can't—"

He put his hand over my mouth to stop me from jabbering on. Then he placed his right arm around my shoulder and lifted my face to meet his with his left hand.

"I want to kiss you," he said, "but I would never disrespect you or want you to do something that neither of us is ready for." Then, with a smile, he added, "Besides, I would have to kill your brother."

Suddenly, there was a downpour of rain that only the south can produce. I slipped out of my shoes and lay my head on Marshall's lap. He began stroking my hair. Enjoying the warmth of the fireplace, I nestled my body deeper into his lap. I allowed him to turn me to face him, his eyes searching mine, my skin tingling as he gently brought my face up to meet his. His mouth began gracefully touching my slightly parted lips. Then his tongue slowly penetrated my mouth, roaming and exploring. Our breaths formed into one. It was hours before we came up for air.

"I have to go," I said reluctantly.

"Now?" he asked sadly.

Nodding, I stood up, slipped into my shoes, and walked to the door. Marshall followed. When we reached Aunt Minnie's, I turned to say goodbye. He wrapped me in his arms and gave me a passionate kiss. I didn't resist, although I could see Phyllis and Melissa peering out the window.

Marshall pushed the door open and playfully said, "I'll see you tomorrow. And by the way, tell your two spies I said goodnight!"

As soon as the door shut behind me, Phyllis and Melissa jumped out from their hiding places. Phyllis wanted to know all the details. As I described the evening to them, Melissa started making gagging noises, as if she were going to throw up. Phyllis and I looked at her, puzzled by her attitude.

"I'm sorry," Melissa said, shaking her head, "I just *can't* imagine anyone thinking Marshall is sexy. Yuck!"

Phyllis said, "Just think about that guy at the movies all the girls were swooning over. Close your eyes and pretend Marshall's not your brother."

Melissa looked at me. "I really want to share this experience with you," she said. "You're my best friend. But just don't say his name, and I'll pretend it's someone else."

I was disappointed. "Is it really that hard?" I asked.

She thought about it a moment. "Let me see if I can explain how I feel," she said at last. "What if I told you that I was just French-kissing Walter and found him irresistible?"

"Oh, no!" I exclaimed, making a face. "I could *never* imagine you with Walter. Okay, I get your point. Then, just imagine it's a complete stranger."

"Yeah!" she added teasingly. "That's the only way I'll get to enjoy the juicy details."

The rest of the summer was filled with exciting activities. Melissa, Phyllis, and I were as close as sisters and shared everything. Melissa had a crush on a boy who worked at the local Dairy Bell, so we ate there until he finally asked her out.

Aunt Minnie's backyard shared a fence with her neighbor, Mrs. Johnson, whose grandson was openly infatuated with Phyllis and was at her beck and call.

We also did a lot of things with the whole family. Walter finally brought his girlfriend around one day. She was very friendly, but reserved and quiet.

Marshall and I had our stolen moments. He was so adoring that I had to learn not to be overwhelmed by his open displays of affection.

Finally, the last weekend was coming, and I was dreading it. Spence had agreed to take us back home because Dad was still out at sea. We had three more days together and were determined to make the most of them.

On Friday, there was a dance at the community center, and we were all going. I decided to wear the outfit that Phyllis and Sandra had bought me, and to fix up my hair, which was very easy to manage now that I had had my hair relaxed.

Putting on the earrings that Marshall had given me, I stepped back to take a look in the mirror. For the first time in my life, I felt good about the way I looked. Phyllis running into the room said, "Everyone's waiting, and..." she stopped in mid-sentence and slowly walked around me, her eyes looking me up and down.

"Is something wrong?" I asked, getting worried. "Is it too much?"

She shook her head, looking mystified. Finally, she said, "No, you look great! Just wait till Marshall sees you!"

I headed down the back stairs, with Phyllis right behind me. Everyone was standing around in the kitchen, eating snacks that Aunt Minnie had prepared. As I walked in, Marshall's face lit up.

"You look *stunning*!" he said, eagerly walking over to me with a big smile.

Stunning?!

This was just like a romance novel. No one had ever told me before that I looked stunning.

I've gotta put this in my diary!

In the middle of my daydreams, I suddenly realized that Aunt Minnie was standing right in front of me with some finger sandwiches.

"Take these and eat them in the car," she said. "You're thin as a bone and haven't had dinner. But I see what took you so long getting dressed."

She let out one of her little giggles.

Marshall and I got into his car, along with Phyllis, Melissa, and their boyfriends, while Walter and Pat and their dates went with Joyce and Spence.

This was my very first dance, and I was so happy to be sharing it with Marshall. We had so much fun. Everyone danced with everyone else, and when the dance was over we didn't want the night to end.

Someone told Walter about a moonlight beach party, so we headed for the beach. When we got there, we could see specks of light. Someone had built a small fire in the sand, and everyone was sitting around drinking soda, roasting marshmallows, and singing.

Marshall ran back to his car to get a blanket from the trunk. When he came back, he spread it out over the sand, close to the fire. We all bunched up in pairs. Marshall and I sat clinging to each other, and spoke very little for the rest of the evening. I didn't want to think about the next day.

When I woke up in the morning and went downstairs to the kitchen, Marshall and Walter were already up and dressed, and were telling Aunt Minnie about the dance and the rest of the evening.

"Good morning," I said with a yawn.

Seeing Marshall put a big smile on my face.

The smell of fresh coffee drew me over to the stove, where I poured myself a cup. This was another luxury that I would soon have to repress. Aunt Minnie let us drink coffee openly, but Mamie would never allow it—although, of course, she was an avid coffee drinker herself. Usually I could sneak a cup on the weekends, when she was gone. I loved coffee. Mother once told me that I would sit with Granny and drink coffee when I was barely able to walk. But I quickly put this memory out of my mind, because I couldn't afford the comfort of dwelling on the past.

Aunt Minnie motioned for me to sit in the chair between her and Marshall. As I ate my breakfast, everyone else trickled into the kitchen and joined us at the table. The mood in the room was somewhat somber.

After breakfast, with great reservation, we all began to pack for the next day's journey "home." Aunt Minnie went from room to room, giving us last-minute tips about how to deal with life, especially Mamie.

"What doesn't kill you will make you stronger," she would say.

But she could hardly talk to me, because, as usual, I was crying my eyes out.

As she sat down on my bed, I was down on the floor trying to close my suitcase. When she spoke to me, I could hear a weariness in her voice. Suddenly, becoming afraid that I might never see her again, I got up and sat on the bed beside her.

"I'll come back and take care of you," I said softly. "You will never have to worry."

"I know," she said, rubbing my arm. "But first you have to take care of yourself." Then, with a smile, she added, "Anyway, I can live off of love."

Looking her in the eyes, I said, "You know very well what I mean."

Aunt Minnie had once told us about a lady who had no children and ended up dying alone. She had been buried in a plain pine box furnished by the state, without any family members attending her funeral. I knew that was one of Aunt Minnie's greatest fears. It's probably one of the reasons she raised my dad.

Getting up, she mumbled, "Enough of all this fuss! You'll be back here before you can shake a leg."

I spent the rest of the day with Melissa and Phyllis. That night I stayed over at Marshall's house. Walter assured Aunt Minnie that he would be there the whole time—and anyway, she could trust me.

Marshall and I talked into the wee hours of the night on the sofa in the living room. Finally, I fell asleep. When I opened my eyes the next morning, it was still dark, and I had forgotten where I was.

"I'm right here," Marshall whispered, hearing me sitting up on the sofa. "You fell asleep."

There was just enough light for me to see that he was lying on the floor nearby.

Pulling up my blanket, I lay back down, remembering our conversation the night before. Then I felt for something around my neck.

It's there!

Marshall had given me his class ring. He had put it on a chain and fastened it around my neck. Holding on to it, I felt so safe and so lucky to have him as a friend. Thinking about our future, I drifted off to sleep.

The next thing I knew, I felt a hand lightly stroking my face. I opened my eyes and looked up, trying to focus. Marshall was staring down at me, looking solemn. I immediately realized what day it was.

Walter came downstairs.

"Aunt Minnie's waiting for us," he said. "Breakfast is ready."

As he helped me up, Marshall said, "Aunt Minnie's trying to fatten me up."

"It's her answer to world peace," I said. "A full belly and a good night's sleep."

After breakfast, we all went out to sit on the front porch. The later it got, the gloomier our mood got. Seeing Spence's car pull up to the front of the house was like watching a hearse arrive to take us to a funeral.

Marshall grabbed my hand and said, "Come with me."

We walked upstairs to my room, and we exchanged again the promises we had made the night before. Naturally, my eyes began to fill with tears. He kissed them away, but more tears immediately took their place. Then we had our private goodbye kiss.

When we went back downstairs, I gave Melissa a big hug, and Walter had to literally pull us apart.

As we drove away in Spence's car, Marshall looked so sad.

13

She's Come Undone

The ride home was quiet. I closed my eyes and imagined what it would be like if I were going back home to Mother.

Would I be safer in her home with my stepfather around?

When we pulled up to the house around seven o'clock, Mamie was standing at the front door. She let Spence and Phyllis go past her, but the rest of us had to go around to the back. She didn't know that Phyllis had spent the summer with us, and probably figured that she had just gone on the ride with Spence to pick us up.

"Thank you so much for bringing them home," Mamie said to Spence. "Sorry you can't stay, but they have to get to bed. We have a long day tomorrow."

When Spence and Phyllis were gone, Mamie turned her attention to us.

"You all go sit at the dining room table," she commanded.

She was plainly on edge. Before speaking, she cleared her throat and sucked on her dentures. Then, pretending to be casual, she began.

"Your dad will be here tomorrow. He's been reassigned to Hawaii. You have three days to make sure all your belongings are packed and ready to be shipped."

With that, she abruptly got up from the table and started to walk away. But then she turned around and said in a threatening tone, "No one is to know about this move. And I mean *no one!*"

At that moment, a car pulled into the driveway, blowing its horn. I immediately knew it was "Cousin" George.

Grabbing her coat, Mamie yelled out, "I'll be back. Start packing!" Just before going out the door, she shouted to Pat, "Get Joseph out of the tub and put him to bed."

No one moved. We just sat there, frozen in our seats with a feeling of immense despair.

I stood up, shaking and trying to choke away my tears and clear my mind.

Maybe someone can help. I'll call Phyllis.

The moment I heard her voice, I burst into tears.

Pat took the phone and told Phyllis what was happening. When she went to the bathroom to get Joseph, Walter called Spence to tell him the story.

While this was happening, Joyce ran into the bathroom and turned on the faucet full blast. She never wanted us to see her crying, but we could hear her sobs over the noise of the running water.

Within minutes, Phyllis, Sandra, and Ernest came rushing in through the front door. Shortly after that, Spence arrived.

We begged Joyce to come out of the bathroom, but she just kept crying.

Finally, Spence picked the lock and let Pat go in first to make sure Joyce was decent. It took him twenty minutes to persuade her to join the rest of us.

I was panicked to see Joyce so distraught. She was always the strong one.

"I'll come and get you when you turn eighteen," Spence said to her. "That's not even a year away. Just wait for me."

She nodded sadly.

We knew that Dad would be coming home the next morning, and we hoped we'd be able to find a way to get our new address from him. From the calendar in the kitchen, we knew that Mamie had a doctor's appointment on Wednesday morning. I would then get the information to Phyllis, and she would pass it on to Marshall and Melissa.

The next morning, I was awakened by loud shouting. Sitting up in bed, I recognized Dad's and Mamie's voices coming from their bedroom. The tyrant must have come home in the middle of the night while we were all sleeping.

"I'll leave you, sell this house, and stay with my sister!" she threatened.

I prayed that she would live up to her words.

But, as usual, Dad caved in to her, and she finally agreed to come with him.

I went to the bathroom to wash up, and when I came out, Joyce, Pat, and Walter were waiting to take their turn. Hearing us stirring about, Dad came out of his bedroom.

"Why do we have to move to Hawaii?" I asked. "And what about our school? Do they have the same schools over there?"

At that time, I thought everyone in Hawaii wore hula skirts and lived in grass shacks.

"It's an emergency," Dad said. "But you'll be able to go to school as soon as we get to the island. Make sure to pack everything you want, because the movers will be here in a few hours to pick up the boxes."

I ran to my bedroom and boxed all the clothes I had from the summer. I kept Marshall's ring around my neck, hiding it under my clothes. Mamie always made us girls button up our blouses to our necks.

When the movers came and hauled all our belongings away, this was my last shred of hope.

Mamie had Joyce and Pat put white sheets over all the furniture, and ordered Walter to nail all the windows shut.

I went with Dad and Joseph to rent a luggage carrier for the top of the car.

When we were away from Mamie, I said to Dad, "I have to show you something, but don't get mad."

He gave me a quick look.

I pulled back my hair, exposing my earrings hanging from my pierced earlobes.

He looked shocked.

"*All* the girls do it," I said. "And besides, Aunt Minnie gave us permission."

"Who's *us*?"

"Me and Pat."

He sighed.

"This is really bad timing," he said. "I'm already in the doghouse."

"I like 'em," Joseph said.

I smiled. "See, Dad. It's *in*."

After a long pause, he said, "Okay. But let *me* deal with your mama."

When we got back to the house, Mamie had us all strip our beds down to the mattress, and then she told me to pour baking powder on the mattresses to keep away the insects and absorb any odors.

I guess we'll be sleeping on the floor tonight, I thought.

We worked until midnight packing up, cleaning, and locking down. By the time all our bags were inside the luggage carrier and in the trunk of the car, everyone was exhausted.

But then Dad announced, "Let's go!"

Joyce looked stunned.

"I thought Mama said we were leaving in two more days," she whined.

Dad looked at us all compassionately, shaking his head.

"Yes," he said, "our plane leaves from California on Friday, but first we have to drive the car to the military base so they can ship it, and we'll fly from there."

Dad had me sit next to him in the front seat, in between him and Maime. Joseph sometimes sat on Mamie's lap and sometimes sat in the back with Joyce, Pat, and Walter. I had mastered reading maps, so Dad wanted my help.

I didn't want Mamie to see that my ears were pierced, so I kept pulling my hair over the sides of my face. Before we left, Pat and Joyce had made me take the earrings off, and Pat put brown thread through my ears to keep the holes from closing. Also, brown would blend in with my skin color. But then, on the second day, it was so hot and muggy in the car that I forgot about my ears and pulled my hair back into a braid.

Mamie started screaming, "What's that hanging from your ears?"

As I touched my ears, my eyes filled with tears. But before I could say anything, Dad spoke up.

"Aunt Minnie told me she was gonna get the girls' hair done at her salon. And she said one of her hair dressers was trying out a new service. I didn't know it was ear piercing until it was already done. I thought it had something to do with hair."

No one said a word. I was shocked but pleased that Dad had told such a big lie to protect us.

Mamie just peered at him. I knew she wanted to lash out at him, but she also wanted to maintain the illusion that she and Dad were always on the same side... against us.

Finally, she said, "Well, we won't have to worry about Minnie interfering for a while."

After that, the trip was relatively peaceful, except Dad got worn out from having to do all the driving, with only a few naps here and there. When we got past the Rockies, he told me there were moments in the mountains that he was so tired he thought he was going to take us over the side.

On Friday afternoon, just a couple of hours before our plane was scheduled to take off, we arrived at Travis Air Force base, totally exhausted.

Dad dropped us off at the waiting area and drove away to make arrangements for the car.

Joyce immediately excused herself to go to the restroom. When she was gone ten minutes, Mamie said to me, "Where's your sister? Go get her!"

I found Joyce down the hall from the restroom.

"Where have you been?" I demanded. "Mamie wants you!"

"I called Spence, "she said, "but he wasn't home or at work, so I called Phyllis. They knew something had happened, because Spence had gone to the house every day, and no one answered. I promised Phyllis we would call them with the address as soon as we get settled."

"Okay," I said, "but you better make up a good story for Mamie why you were away so long."

Although I was leaving all my friends behind and Aunt Minnie too, I was actually looking forward to the adventure of flying. I think we all were, except for Mamie who was obviously jittery but trying to hide it.

Joseph was constantly asking her questions about how high we were going to fly, and how long it would take, and who was "driving" the plane, when suddenly she snapped at him, "Sit here and be quiet!"

Walter and I looked at each other knowingly. We had never seen Mamie talk to her little prince like that.

Joseph wasn't used to it either, and so, he started crying.

Pat walked over, taking him by the hand, and said to him, "Come on, Junior, let's go to the bathroom before we get on the plane."

Mamie looked a little guilty as she watched them walk away.

When Dad showed up, it was time to board the plane.

He and Mamie sat in the front of the plane with Joseph, and the rest of us sat together in the back. I sat next to a window on the left side, with Walter to my right and an empty seat between us. Across the aisle, Joyce and Pat sat together with a stranger at their window.

I looked out with anticipation, excited to take off. Then the four of us started talking so much that the next thing I knew, we were up in the air. Once we left land behind, there was so much water! It made me feel peaceful.

After a while, the stewardess came around with a tray offering drinks. Everyone took a soda pop except me. With Mamie safely in the front, I ordered a coffee.

But despite the caffeine and the excitement of flying for the first time, I soon fell into a deep sleep. I was exhausted from helping Dad with the navigation as he drove.

"Wake up, we're landing!" Walter said, nudging me.

I looked out the window and saw the most beautiful blue water and white sand beaches I had ever seen in my life.

When we landed, we were met by a driver, who took us in a military car to our temporary housing on the base. I was overwhelmed by how green everything was, with flowers and fruit growing wild everywhere.

We stayed in an apartment on the base for the first week. We couldn't go anywhere off the base, because we didn't have our car. However, there were beaches all around, so Joyce, Walter, Pat, and I usually went swimming all day. Sometimes we took Joseph with us, and sometimes he stayed behind. We would pack sandwiches and eat the fruit right off the trees—bananas, mangos, pineapples, and coconuts. It was like being in the Garden of Eden.

Throughout that week, Mamie mostly stayed on her bed, sulking. We didn't think about it then, but she was probably missing "Cousin" George.

Eventually, Dad found us a townhouse in Waipahu, twenty minutes away. One of Mamie's conditions was that we not live on the base, because she felt that base housing was not good enough for her.

When we arrived at the townhouse, we dropped our bags and ran through the place. The entrance was on the upper floor, which had the master bedroom and bathroom, two smaller bedrooms, a living room, a kitchen, and a large main bathroom. A stairway by the front door led down to the lower level, where there were two more bedrooms, a bathroom, and a family room.

We had no beds yet, so Dad and Mamie slept in their room on a mattress on the floor. Walter slept in one of the downstairs bedrooms on a floor mattress, and Joyce, Pat, and I slept in the other downstairs bedroom, sharing one big mattress. Joseph had his own mattress in one of the upstairs bedrooms, but he was afraid to sleep alone in a new place, so he slept with Dad and Mamie.

That arrangement went on for four or five days until someone told Dad about a military family a few doors down that was moving out and selling all their furniture. I arranged with Joyce, Pat, and Walter that I would take a room upstairs near Mamie, Dad, and Joseph in exchange for getting the biggest mattress. Thus, I ended up with a double bed, Joyce and Pat got twin beds, and Walter got a captain's bed—a twin bed with drawers under it. We later realized that the space behind those drawers was great for hiding things.

On Friday, Dad took us over to our schools to get us registered. Starting on Monday, Joyce, Pat, and Walter would be going to Waipahu High School, and I would be going to Waipahu Junior High.

While we were filling out the forms, Mamie stayed at home. She was still so upset about having to leave Virginia, and hated everything about Hawaii so much, that she just stayed in the bedroom for hours at a time. Dad tried to cheer her up by taking her out shopping, but she spent most of her time being depressed.

Her hibernation was a wonderful vacation for us. And we *loved* Hawaii! Dad loved it, too. The people were so warm and friendly, with such a laid-back style, that we didn't feel out of place from the moment we got there.

After we were in the townhouse about a week, the phone company came out and connected the lines. Now we would have a chance to sneak in some collect calls to Aunt Minnie and our friends back home.

As I was sitting outside one day, I saw a black girl about my own age walk out of a nearby unit. I waved, and she came over smiling.

"Hi," she said, "my name is Pat. What's yours?"

"Just call me Reesa," I said. "I have a sister named Pat."

"Oh! In that case, you can call me PK. That's what my family calls me. How many people are in your family?"

"I have two sisters and two brothers. I'm the next to the youngest. How about you?"

After pausing for a moment, she said, "Well, I have two sisters now...it's a long story." She smiled. Then, looking puzzled, she asked, "Is that lady your mom?"

Looking around to make sure Mamie was nowhere in sight, I shook my head.

"No," I said, "she's my stepmother." Then I whispered, "And she's *very* mean."

We chatted for a while, and discovered that we would be in the same grade together.

When I set out for school the next morning, PK was waiting for me.

"Let's go before we're late!" she hollered.

Without Mamie breathing down my neck, I had lost track of time.

Twenty minutes later, when we got to school, PK and I went to our separate homerooms. When I walked into mine, I was amazed to see that half of the students weren't wearing shoes.

There was a beautiful Samoan girl across the room in my homeroom class. I kept staring at her because her skin was flawless, and she had jet black hair that fell down past her waist. After a while, every time I looked up, I saw that she was glaring at me.

When the bell rang for us to go to our next class, she walked over and said with a sour expression on her face, "You like beef, eh?"

I was puzzled. Thinking that she might be inviting me to lunch, I said, "Yes, I like beef."

She pointed outside to the entrance of the school.

"After school," she said, "you like beef. . . I like beef."

"Okay," I said, trying to give a little smile. But she seemed so serious.

At the end of the school day, I was waiting for my new friend at the entrance when she showed up with two other girls. All three were looking hostile.

The beautiful girl handed one of the others her schoolbooks and walked directly up to me and said right in my face, "You still like beef, eh?"

"Sure," I said.

With that, she punched me right in the nose.

Blood began running down my face. Dropping my books, I covered my nose and started screaming, "What did you do that for?"

Until that moment, I hadn't realized that a crowd had formed around us. Then I heard Walter's voice.

"Move! Let me through!"

Looking bewildered he asked, "What happened?"

The Samoan girl yelled, "She like beef with me!"

"What?" Walter exclaimed, taking his shirt off and putting it up to my nose.

Suddenly, a Samoan boy about Walter's age walked up to the girl and started questioning her. Then he turned to Walter and they walked away from the crowd and started talking. After a minute, Walter and the boy walked back together.

Walter grabbed my hand and pulled me away from the crowd toward the Samoan girl and boy.

"Hi," the boy said. "My name is Ka'ai. This is my sister, Makai."

I stood there fuming at her. By now I was ready to fight!

"My sister said you were staring at her all through homeroom," Ka'ai said. "She asked if you wanted to fight with her, and you said yes."

"No, I didn't!" I exclaimed. "She asked me if I liked beef, and I said yes."

Ka'ai laughed.

"Beef! That's the native word for fight. She was asking if you had a beef with her."

"Oh, wow!" I said. "We're fresh from the mainland, and I don't know the native language. I was staring at her because I thought she was beautiful. But now I wanna fight her!"

Makai walked over and extended her hand.

"I'm sorry," she said. "What's your name?"

Shaking her hand, I replied, "Just call me Reesa."

As she walked away with her brother, she called out to me, "I'll see you in homeroom tomorrow!"

When I got home, I told Joyce and Pat what had happened at school, and they found it very funny.

The next day, Makai was waiting for me outside homeroom, holding a beautiful white lei. As she handed it to me, she said, "Peace offering."

"Thank you," I said, putting it around my neck.

"I'll come get you at lunch," she said, "and you can hang out with me and my friends. Besides, I need to teach you some native language before you *really* get in trouble."

We both laughed.

After that, PK, Makai, and I became great friends.

Walter was in heaven in Hawaii. He especially loved seeing all the fresh fruit growing on trees everywhere. Soon after we moved into the townhouse, he got a job as a bagger and a stock boy at a supermarket just a few blocks away. When he cashed his first paycheck, Mamie took most of the money, but he managed to sneak a few dollars in change out of his tips so we could call home.

Joyce really wanted to call Spence, so she told Mamie that she and I were going over to the supermarket to get some milk. At the pay phone outside the supermarket, she tried to call, but Spence's number was disconnected. I suggested that she try the restaurant, but they put her on hold and made her wait so long that her money ran out.

As we walked home, Joyce looked really sad.

"We'll try again soon," I assured her.

Soon after this, the assistant minister at the local community church left, so Dad had our pastor back in Virginia write him a letter of recommendation, and that was enough to get Dad the job.

It took Mamie a while to warm up to the church because it was so different from our church back in Virginia. There was a lot of focus on young people, and the congregation was not starchy and stuck up like the one back home. However, once Dad was appointed the Assistant Pastor, she felt important and wanted to be seen.

Mamie didn't care about the townhouse the way she did about the house in Virginia, so she wasn't constantly pestering us about it. Nevertheless, we were so conditioned that we kept the place immaculate anyway. Joyce more or less took over the job of assigning us chores.

Early one Saturday afternoon, Joyce was walking around looking so gloomy that when Mamie went out to do a little shopping, I picked up the phone in the kitchen and called Phyllis's house collect. Sandra answered and accepted the charges. I apologized for calling collect, explaining that we had no money. She assured me that it was fine.

Hearing me on the phone, Joyce picked up the extension in Mamie's bedroom.

"Sandra," she cut in, "I've been trying to call Spence, but his phone is disconnected, and I haven't been able to reach him at the restaurant."

"Ernest says he looks like a sick puppy," Sandra said. "He was calling me every day to see if I'd heard from you. But then, last week, his mom up in New Jersey got ill, and he went home to check on her. I haven't heard from him since. Ernest says the people at the restaurant don't think he's coming back."

Joyce was so distraught that she hung up without saying goodbye.

"Is she okay?" Sandra asked.

"She's really sad, but we'll take care of her... Could I speak to Phyllis?"

"She went out to dinner and a movie with some friends."

"In the middle of the afternoon?"

"It's six o'clock here, honey."

"Oh, I forgot about the time difference. Well, tell Phyllis I'll write to her and send her an address where she can reach me."

PK and I had already arranged for her to get my mail.

When I hung up, I looked for Joyce. She was sitting in the living room looking totally heartbroken.

14

Joyce

It was weeks after that before Joyce came out of her depression. Eventually, she joined the youth group at the church and threw herself into helping troubled kids.

The youth minister, whose name was Tommy, kept pursuing her, but she avoided his advances. Among Pentecostals at that time, there was no such thing as casual dating. You only went out with someone you considered a possible marriage prospect. And Joyce was still grieving over Spence.

But after working with Tommy at the church for a while, she got to like him and agreed to go out with him. First, however, he had to get my dad's permission. That was no problem, but Mamie insisted that they could only go out if someone were with them. That "someone" usually turned out to be me, but we found ways to get around it.

Before long, Joyce and Tommy were an item. They were always going out or working together on church projects. It was so nice to see her happy again.

We never heard from Spence. Later we learned from Ernest that he never came back to Virginia after his mother died.

It only took us a few months to get used to living on the island. Dad was home now more than he used to be. Or rather, he wasn't at sea. But he spent most of his free hours at the church.

Mamie joined a women's social club that held weekly meetings and often went off on shopping trips. She was forced to treat us a little better because she was a lot more dependent on us now than she had been on the mainland, where she had her sister, friends, and boyfriend to support her. Her illiteracy, in particular, was more of a handicap here. And she probably was afraid that the police wouldn't be so lenient about physically disciplining kids as they were in the South. There were still spurts of abuse from her, but life was much better for us.

Joseph had things slightly worse than before because Mamie still treated him like a baby. She insisted on walking him to school, even though it was only five minutes away and all the other kids his age went alone.

Walter took a lot of morning classes so he could spend most of his day at work. I envied how he got perfect grades with little or no effort. In fact, after taking the assessment tests, he skipped over a whole year and was now in the same grade as Pat, who was a year older.

Unlike the rest of us, Pat was a party animal. She was on an island full of servicemen and had discovered that she could slip out of her bedroom window without being detected. She would slip out almost every weekend. Just in case Mamie came downstairs to check on her, she would place pillows under her blanket and a scarf over the top. This was very risky, but she didn't seem to care anymore and was becoming openly defiant.

I was also beginning to explore my newfound freedom. On the way to school every morning, I would stop at a gas station, go into the restroom, and go through a complete physical transformation. First, I would slip off my shoes and put them in my book bag. Then I would put on lip gloss and mascara. And finally, I would pull my blouse out and roll my skirt up at the waist, turning it into a miniskirt.

Before long, PK and I were cutting school and going to the beach at least once a week. We didn't worry about the school sending notices home, because PK had shown us all how to pick the locks on the mailboxes, and we would take out anything we wanted.

One day, as PK and I were heading home from the beach, before we got to the gas station for my reverse transformation, Dad's car pulled up alongside us, and he beckoned for us to get in.

As we drove along, no one said a word. After dropping PK off, Dad drove a few blocks away from our townhouse and pulled over to the side of the road.

"How long have you been drinking?" he asked solemnly.

Tears welled up in my eyes. I didn't want to lie to him.

"Only a couple of times," I said, choking between sobs. "How did you know?"

Dad didn't answer. He just drove to the beach and walked me to the caves where PK and I would hang out. Our empty beer cans were lying all around, and so were cans of spray paint, because every time we cut school, we would spray our names and the date on the walls.

"*That's* how," he said. "My unit patrols this side of the island. Some girls have been raped on this beach, so we've been keeping our eye on it. Can you imagine my shock and disappointment when I found your name plastered all over these walls?"

I just sat there in disbelief.

How could I have been so stupid?

"Get back to the car!" he ordered.

We drove back to the base, and Dad parked in front of the officers' club. Then he came around and opened my door, and motioned for me to get out. I followed him into the club. Everyone was saluting him and stepping out of our way.

Dad walked up to a round table and pulled out a chair.

"Sit down!" he commanded.

As I did, he walked around to the chair across from me and sat down, beckoning to the waitress. She came over with a big smile.

"Johnny Walker Red with a coke," he said, "and a cola."

Wow! I've never seen Dad drink before!

When the waitress came back, she gave me the cola and Dad the liquor. He handed her a hundred dollar bill and said, "Keep it coming."

I reached for the cola, but Dad grabbed it and pushed the liquor in front of me.

"Drink it!" he snapped.

I took a sip. It tasted awful, but I kept sipping it because I didn't want him to be mad. Before I finished the drink, the waitress was back with another round. This time she put the drinks in the middle of the table. She and everyone else near that table knew what was going on.

I only remember getting midway through the third drink.

Everything after that is a blank. Sometime the next day, I woke up feeling as if I had fallen off a cliff. Looking around, I had no idea where I was. When I tried to raise my head, the room was spinning around.

"How's your stomach?" a familiar female voice said.

It was Sister Linda from our church.

I was too nauseous to answer.

"Let's get you to the bathtub," she said.

As she helped me to get up, I saw a bucket of vomit on the floor next to the bed. The whole room reeked of vomit and sweat.

Somehow, she got me into that tub, and as I lay back in the warm water, I watched her strip all the sheets off the bed. After I had soaked for awhile, Sister Linda came in with some fresh clothes for me.

After getting dressed, I walked slowly out of the bathroom, holding on to the walls. Sister Linda and Dad were sitting at a table in the kitchen down the hallway. I could smell the aroma of fresh coffee.

When I walked into the kitchen, Sister Linda smiled and said, "Sit down."

As I did, she came over to me with a glass in her hand and put it down in front of me. Sipping it, I recognized some kind of concoction of tomato juice and only God knows what else.

Gently rubbing my head, she said, "Drink up. It looks awful, but it'll make you feel better."

Returning to her seat, she gave Dad a soft touch on the shoulder.

"Joseph," she said, "you should be ashamed of yourself."

I glanced at her with surprise.

I think she just slipped. She always calls him "Reverend" at church.

We all pretended that nothing was going on.

Dad jumped up and tugged at the back of my chair.

"Okay," he said, "let's go. We've overstayed our welcome."

Mamie was standing at the front door looking pissed when we arrived home.

"Where have you been all night?" she hollered at me, staring me right in the face.

"I, uh . . ."

Dad pushed me through the door.

"We've been at the church," he said, "fasting and praying."

My mouth dropped wide open.

Pat walked up to me, clapped her hand over my mouth, and led me downstairs.

"What in the heck's going on?" Joyce inquired when I walked into their bedroom.

I poured out the whole story to them, including the part about Sister Linda. When I was done, we all sat there overwhelmed by the turn of events.

Later that day, when Mamie was out of the way, I promised Dad that there would be no more cutting school or drinking. In return, he said he would let me spend most of my time with PK.

In a month or so, my school was going to be putting on a talent show. PK and I signed up for it, along with Makai and a girl named Jackie. The four of us met every day at PK's townhouse. I told Mamie we were preparing for a science project, but we were actually practicing to lip-sync a song, pretending to be Diana Ross and the Supremes. I would be Diana, because I had very big eyes and was skinny, and people often said I looked like her. Jackie and PK would play the Supremes. Makai, who was a terrific dancer, was our coach. Her mother was a seamstress, so she made our costumes.

Everyone's parents would be coming to the show but mine since I had told Mamie and Dad that I was involved in a science project. I told the other girls that Dad couldn't come because he had some obligation at the church. They knew better than to ask about Mamie.

On the evening of the show, I went straight to PK's after school. Makai did our makeup and hair. Then I slipped into my dress and went over to look at myself in the mirror.

"Wow!" I exclaimed, touching my hair.

My blue dress was floor-length with a slit up the front all the way to my thighs. My accessories were royal blue rhinestone earrings and long black gloves. PK and Jackie each had the exact same dress, but in black, with long black gloves and black rhinestone earrings. Our shoes were identical: three-inch heels with pointed toes.

We walked perfectly in them because Makai had made us rehearse in them every day for a month.

PK's mom drove us over to the school, and we all went backstage to get ready. I knew that Pat and Walter were out in the audience. Joyce wasn't there because she was doing something at the church.

I was getting butterflies in my stomach, but Jackie and Makai kept telling me that they had a big surprise for me.

Finally, we heard the announcer introduce our group.

Makai ran out front so she could see every move.

As I walked out on stage, I looked around to see where Pat and Walter were. Sitting right next to them was Dad!

I was so shocked that my mouth flew wide open. Thank God, our routine called for us to turn our backs to the audience until the music started.

PK saw the tears in my eyes, and whispered, "Don't you dare drop a tear on this stage!"

The music started, and we turned around, doing our rendition of "Stop in the Name of Love."

I was perfect, but the whole time I was thinking, "You are so dead!"

The moment the routine was over, I ran off the stage, but Dad was waiting for me in the wings. I kept my head down, unable to look at him. Walking over to me, he put his arms around my shoulders.

"You were great!" he said. "I'm only sorry you didn't think you could tell me."

I started crying so hard that I didn't hear them call our group. Then PK and Jackie ran over and dragged me onstage.

"We won first place!" they screamed.

When everything had settled down, Dad gave me permission to spend the night at PK's.

One Saturday in June, when we had been in Hawaii about ten months, Joyce came home in the afternoon and said she had an announcement to make. We all had a pretty good idea what it was.

A moment later, the doorbell rang, and Joyce opened the door. To no one's surprise, it was Tommy. He and Joyce had been dating about six months by this time. She grabbed his hand and led him to the dining room.

When we were all assembled there, Tommy said, "Reverend Armstrong, I would like to ask you for permission to marry your daughter, sir!"

I was smiling from ear to ear.

"Welcome to the family," Dad said.

"I know you'll take good care of my sister, man," Walter said, shaking his hand.

"Where are you getting married?" Pat asked.

"At the church," Joyce said.

"When?" I asked.

"What am *I* gonna do?" Joseph asked.

"Wait a minute!" Joyce said. "Relax! We'll tell you all the details."

Mamie suddenly turned around and walked out of the room. A moment later, we heard the bedroom door slam. Apparently, she couldn't stand to be around so much happiness.

Joyce put her head down, embarrassed for Tommy's sake, but he walked over, lifted her chin, and gave her a smile.

Pat walked into the kitchen and came back with seven cocktail glasses filled with 7-Up. I was thinking that Mamie would kill her if she found out we were using her good glasses.

"Drink up everybody, this is a celebration," Pat said sarcastically, glancing toward Mamie's door.

Dad had a toast with us and then went groveling to Mamie. We could hear them arguing, but couldn't quite make out the words. The best we could figure was that Mamie was upset over having to spend money on the wedding.

After Tommy left, Joyce went over all the details with us. She would be graduating in three weeks and was preparing for the wedding sometime in August.

"Pastor Mark is checking dates in August for us," she said. "Tommy's gotten orders from the Navy that he'll only be here in

Honolulu one more year, and then he's gonna be stationed in D.C. In the meantime, his apartment's big enough for the two of us."

Over the next few weeks, Mamie was so mean to Joyce that it seemed Joyce couldn't do anything right. Mamie was constantly scolding her and making excuses to keep her and Tommy apart.

Finally, the school year ended, and I had mixed feelings because, on the one hand, I was looking forward to Joyce's wedding, but, on the other hand, I wouldn't be able to spend the summer at Aunt Minnie's. When I called Phyllis to let her know I wouldn't be coming, she was disappointed but understood.

"What are you gonna do about Marshall?" she asked.

"I'll call him in a week or two when I know he and Melissa have arrived. He just graduated, too, and I know he plans to drive up to Elizabeth City. But how about you? What are *you* doing for the summer?"

"Sandra's been trying to get me to do the Black College Tour, so I guess I'll do it now. I'll send you a postcard from each college."

"Great!"

A couple of weeks later, I tried to call Marshall at his grandmother's house in Elizabeth City, but there was no answer, so I called Aunt Minnie. She seemed disoriented and kept switching from one subject to another. At one point, she said something about Miss Pearl, Marshall's grandmother, and how she would miss her. When I asked her why, or where Miss Pearl was, she never quite responded.

I was concerned about Aunt Minnie, and felt that I should go visit her. When I brought this up with Dad, he said, "Reesa Baby, her doctors say she's showing early signs of Alzheimer's disease."

"What's that?"

"When you get older, you start to forget things. But don't worry, she's okay. We've gotta concentrate on the wedding right now."

"You're right, I guess."

"A nurse comes to visit Aunt Minnie a few times a week," he said. "She told me that you promised you would take care of her. When the time comes, I'll make sure you keep that promise."

15

A Way of Escape

For the next several weeks, Joyce, Pat, and I were busy ordering and sending out invitations to the wedding, choosing the cake, picking out flowers, and trying on dresses. Joyce tried on one wedding gown after another, until Pat and I thought she would never pick one. But finally she did. We didn't have to order champagne or a DJ, because Mamie wouldn't allow drinking or dancing. Besides, the reception was at the church hall, and I doubt that Pastor Mark would have allowed dancing or alcohol in the building.

The weekend before the wedding, Joyce went to church for a youth program and didn't come home until a little after midnight. Mamie was waiting for her, and when she saw her pull up in Tommy's car, she was furious because she had a rule that Joyce could not be alone with Tommy, but had to have a chaperone.

I was sleeping upstairs all this time until I was awakened by Mamie's screaming.

"You tramp!"

Then I heard the sound of a belt hitting Joyce's flesh, and Joyce crying out in pain.

"You whore!"

More whipping.

Finally, Joyce yelled, "Nothing happened! I promise, I'm still a virgin."

"For the rest of this week," Mamie screamed, "there will be no phone calls, no contact, no nothin'! You will obey me until you leave this house!"

When I heard Mamie's door slam, I ran downstairs.

Joyce was lying on her bed weeping, and Pat was angrily pacing around the room.

"This is her sadistic way of proving she still has control," Pat yelled.

"Lower your voice," I snapped. Then I walked over to Joyce and covered her with a blanket. "Her goal is to ruin this for Joyce," I said. "We have to stay calm for just six more days, and she'll never be able to touch you again."

"You're right," Joyce said in a voice that was barely a whisper.

I crawled into bed with her and cuddled up next to her until she fell asleep. Then I went back to my room.

The next day, when Tommy called, I told him what happened, and that Mamie had put Joyce on restriction, so he couldn't talk to her.

He was livid.

"I'm coming over there," he said. "Right now!"

"No, wait. Let's talk. I'll come over to the church."

When I got off the phone, I ran downstairs and told Joyce that I was going over to talk to Tommy, because he was threatening to come over.

"Let him come!" Pat said. "It's time *somebody* stood up to her!"

Joyce started crying hysterically just as Walter came in.

"This is not about *you!*" Walter said to Pat. "This is about Joyce. And she wants her wedding."

"Tommy's waiting for me at the church," I said. "We better get over there before he comes *here*."

As the three of us walked to the church, which was about twenty minutes away, I said to Pat and Walter, "We've all worked too hard for Joyce to have her special day, only to let Mamie have the satisfaction of spoiling it now."

When we got to the church, Tommy was pacing around outside. There were people inside, so we walked off a little ways. I could see that Tommy was about to explode.

"I can't take it anymore," he said. "I'll march right in that house and take her out!"

"That would make Mamie perfectly happy," Walter said. "She'd love nothing better than to ruin your wedding. It's only six more days. I suggest that the three of us form a protective shield around

Joyce. At least one of us will be with her at all times. If Mamie tries to find any excuse to hit her, one of us will take the blame."

"I'll go along with that," Tommy said. "But I won't tolerate one more incident."

Thus, for the next six days, we assisted Joyce in all her work and never left her alone. Mamie knew what we were doing, but Pat was so intense that it persuaded even Mamie to back down.

At last, the alarm clock went off on the big day. Not that I needed the alarm because I was waking up every hour with anticipation. I had a big surprise for Joyce.

I jumped out of bed and went to the kitchen. Dad was sitting at the table.

"Hey, Dad," I said, "do you want a cup of coffee?"

Not waiting for an answer, I pulled the coffee can off the shelf and started making a pot. Dad just looked at me. He knew I was making enough for both of us, but he had no objection.

Then Mamie walked in and spoiled my plans.

"Go and make sure your sisters are awake," she ordered, pouring herself my cup of coffee.

When I went downstairs, Joyce and Pat were sitting up in bed talking. I sat down on the side of Pat's bed, which was nearer to the door.

"She just wants to be sure you're both awake," I said.

"Everybody decent?" Dad asked in a teasing way, knocking on the door. When he walked in, he sat down beside me, holding a cup of coffee. Without a word, he handed it to me.

"Thank you," I said, hoarsely gulping the coffee down and handing the empty cup back to him.

He winked, got up and walked over to Joyce, kissed her on the forehead, and went back upstairs.

"Let's go!" I said excitedly, pulling the covers first off Joyce and then off Pat. Half an hour later, we all got into Dad's car and headed to the church. That is, everyone except Mamie. She stayed behind to get dressed. Actually, she was still bitter and angry with Dad for spending money on the wedding.

Walter and Joseph sat in front with Dad. Walter was already dressed in his tuxedo, although he was carrying his jacket. Joyce, Pat, and I sat in back with our dresses in our laps. We would put them on at the church.

As Dad dropped us off, he said, "Joseph and I will be back in an hour with Mama."

"Don't be a moment late, Dad," Joyce said. "You're walking me down the aisle, and Joseph is my ring bearer."

When we stepped into the dressing room at the church, Joyce let out a gasp. The entire room was filled with white roses. We all knew that Joyce loved white roses, so Walter had made a deal with his boss at the supermarket to get a hundred dozen white roses! The night before the wedding, Walter, Pat, and I had met the wholesaler at the church, and covered the whole sanctuary with roses.

Now, as Joyce stood in the dressing room crying, Walter handed her a small box. Joyce was shaking so hard that she could hardly open it. Finally, she pulled out a perfect string of pearls.

Walter took the necklace and placed it around her neck.

Then he leaned in close to her and whispered, "You are the closest thing to a mother we ever had, Sis."

We all began to cry.

A moment later, Makai and PK walked in.

"Hey," PK said with a chuckle, "are we having a wedding here or a funeral?"

Everyone laughed and cried simultaneously.

"Well," Walter said, heading for the door, "I'll go see how Tommy's doing."

Holding up a pressing comb in one hand and an iron in the other, Makai said with a big smile, "I brought *both* pressing combs!"

PK and I couldn't stop laughing.

"What's the joke?" Pat huffed.

"It's a long story," PK said.

"Well," Pat said, "if you're gonna keep carrying on about it, tell us the damn story."

"Okay," I said. "One day, Makai begged me to spend the night at her house, but I kept refusing because I had just shampooed my hair and needed to press it. I hadn't been to a hairdresser since I left the mainland, so I no longer had any chemicals in my hair. Makai said, 'Oh! I thought you had some deep dark secret. Samoan hair is much like yours. It gets really wavy and kinky when it's shampooed. I press my hair, too.' 'Really,' I said. 'Swear to god,' she said, raising her right hand. So I asked Dad if I could spend the night at Makai's, and he said it was okay. The next morning, as I was getting dressed for school, I asked Makai where she kept her pressing comb. She looked at me as if I were speaking a foreign language. 'Hello!' I said. 'The pressing comb. . . to press your hair.' 'Oh, it's in the other room,' she said. 'I was just pressing mine.' So I followed her into the other room, and she walked right up to an ironing board, lay her hair over it, and began to press it with the iron! I was so shocked, I couldn't believe my eyes. For a moment, I literally couldn't speak. But when I did, *she* was stunned. 'How in the hell do you think I'm supposed to put this natural on that ironing board?!' I yelled. 'What could you have *possibly* been thinking? I need a pressing *comb*! Not a darn iron!' Makai looked dumbfounded. But her mother heard us from the next room and said to me, 'How about I take you home to get your comb?' I was so relieved.

"When we got back to Makai's, I showed her and her mother how to use the pressing comb. I pressed Makai's hair first, and she was so delighted with the results that her mother asked me to do her hair. Her mom couldn't believe how silky her hair was. Before we knew it, she had called all her sisters over, and instead of going to school, I spent the entire day pressing the hair of all the women in that family. After school, PK came over and saw all the ladies lined up to get their hair pressed. When I told her how they had been pressing their hair on an ironing board, she was just as amazed as I had been. Pretty soon, I was known on the island as the silk girl, and would spend my weekends at Makai's house pressing hair. The ladies paid me fifteen or twenty dollars each, and I spent most of the money on clothes."

Pat and Joyce laughed at the story.

"I always wondered why Makai's family called you the silk girl," Pat said. "I just thought it was a Samoan name."

We all laughed. Then we got back to the business of preparing Joyce for her wedding. I did her hair while Makai did her makeup. This was the first time Joyce had on something more than lip gloss.

When I placed the veil on her head and turned her to the mirror, tears welled up in her eyes.

"Don't mess up your makeup!" I said, fanning her with my hand and fighting back my own tears.

Joyce reached for her glasses and put them on.

"Oh, no! You can't wear those ugly things," Pat said, waving her hands.

"I don't want to hear *her* mouth," Joyce said with a shrug.

"An hour from now, you'll be a married woman," Pat said. "You're grown up, and it's high time she knows it."

Pat walked over to Joyce, pulled the glasses off her face, and handed them to me.

"Take these," she said, "and don't produce them until I give you the word."

The wedding was beautiful. Joyce was radiant and looked like a princess, and Pat, Walter, and I felt that we were celebrating the liberation of one of us.

By the end of August, I still hadn't been able to reach Marshall and Melissa. No one ever answered the phone.

School was starting in two weeks. Pat and Walter were both excited because this would be their last year. I was excited to be entering my sophomore year at Waipahu High School.

By now, I was spending tons of time at Joyce and Tommy's house. It was like having Sandra and Ernest living a few blocks away all over again. Joyce learned to drive and would pick Pat and me up from school all the time. Mamie didn't complain because she took advantage of Joyce when she wanted to go shopping and Dad wasn't around.

When Pat turned eighteen that December, she started to become even more defiant. Mamie pretended to ignore it, but I was sure she was up to something. The Monday after Pat's birthday, Mamie showed up at our school. She walked into Pat's classroom and loudly asked her teacher about the letter she had sent her, which said that Pat had cut school on her birthday. Then Mamie walked over to Pat's desk and subjected her to a public humiliation in front of the entire class. Pat got up and ran for the door, but Mamie had brought two of the deacons from the church with her. They grabbed Pat, took her to a car, and shoved her in the back seat. Then Mamie sat down on one side of her, and one of the deacons sat down on the other side. She slapped and hit Pat all the way home.

PK came running into my class to tell me what had happened, and I immediately went to Walter's class to get him. As we ran home, Walter was crying. He sounded like a wounded animal. As we charged into Pat's room, she was packing.

"I'm leaving," she said as she snatched clothes out of her closet. "I'm grown, and I won't stay another day."

Walter looked anxious.

"Where will you stay?" he asked.

"I don't know. . . outside if I have to."

Walter ran to his room. I could hear him opening and closing drawers. Then he was back with a duffel bag and a suitcase.

"I have money and a job," he said. "We can get an apartment. I'm going with you."

I started crying.

"What about *me*?" I whined. "I don't wanna stay here."

Pat grabbed me by the arm.

"We'll help you," she said. "But we can't do it if we stay here. If you come with us, she'll call the police. You're a minor."

Walter tried to soothe me.

"I can hide till I'm eighteen, but you can't. And chances are she won't call the police on me. . . I think she's afraid of me."

I knew he was right. Mamie hadn't raised her hand to Walter in over a year.

"Alright," I said, "but you have to promise to call me at Joyce's house tomorrow."

Within a few minutes, they were gone.

About an hour later, I heard Mamie and Dad come in the house, and then she went straight down to Pat's room. A moment later, she rushed upstairs and flung open my door.

"Where are they?" she questioned.

As I glared back at her, I saw Dad walk up behind her.

"They left," I snapped. "Pat said she's grown and doesn't have to stay here anymore."

"Well, Walter's not," she said bitterly. "I'll have the police pick him up."

"You wouldn't dare," I mumbled.

"What did you say?" she yelled, walking toward me threateningly.

I cleared my throat to muster up some courage.

"He said you wouldn't dare do that."

She stopped in her tracks. I could tell she was afraid. As she turned and looked at Dad, he looked so sad, as if he had aged ten years.

"Pat's right," he said. "She doesn't have to live here anymore. No one can make her stay. And as for Walter, I'd rather he was with her. He can look out for her."

Looking downcast, he turned to go.

"I'm tired," he said, dragging himself toward his room.

Mamie followed behind, mumbling her dissent.

Pat never went back to school. Within three days, she had a job as a retail clerk in a local women's clothing store.

Walter, on the other hand, stayed in school. His plan was to join the Army, continue his education, and see the world. He only had six months before graduating. His boss at the market owned an adjacent apartment house in which there was a vacancy, so Walter and Pat moved in there. It was a one-bedroom apartment, so Walter slept on a pullout couch and Pat slept in the bedroom.

Mamie was furious and forbade me to visit their place. Of course, I broke that prohibition as soon as I could, and even had my own key, so I would go over there once or twice a week, usually with PK, to watch TV or just hang out. Half the time, Pat and Walter were at work and weren't even there.

One afternoon when PK and I were over there, I completely lost track of time, so it was around 5:00 P. .M. when I got home, a good two hours later than usual. Naturally, Mamie was waiting for me at the door and started screaming the moment I walked in.

"Do you know your way home?" she asked. "You were supposed

to pick up your little brother from school. He was out there for over an hour, crying his eyes out. What were you *doing*?"

"I forgot."

"*Forgot!* Forgot your little brother?"

"Yes, ma'am. I'm sorry, Joseph."

"I had to get a ride from one of the church members to pick him up. Were you at Pat's house?"

"I...uh..."

She slapped me across the face so hard that I lost my balance. Falling to the floor, I hit my forehead against the coffee table, which sent blood squirting everywhere. I started crying hysterically.

"Joseph!" Mamie yelled. "Go get a towel!"

He ran to the linen closet and came back with a small towel. I put it over my wound, but it wouldn't stop bleeding.

Mamie was pacing back and forth. Finally, she said to Joseph, "Go to PK's house and see if Ivy or someone can take Reesa to the base hospital."

A few minutes later, Joseph came back with Ivy and PK.

"Can you put some ice in a towel?" Ivy said to Mamie.

Mamie ran off to the kitchen and came back with the wrapped ice, which I pressed against my forehead. I was still crying, and I cried all the way to the hospital.

When the doctor asked me what had happened, I said that I had simply slipped and fallen.

Afterward, back in the car on the way home, PK said, "Joseph told us that Mamie slapped you, so why did you lie to the doctor?"

"It was nothing," I said.

"I hate lies," she said. Then, looking at her sister, she added, "Lies really screw up a person."

Ivy threw a nervous glance at me in the rearview mirror.

"Can I tell her?" PK asked.

Ivy nodded as she wiped tears from her cheeks.

PK turned around so that she could look directly into my eyes.

"My little sister is not really my little sister," she said.

"Madison? She's not your sister?"

"No, she's my niece." I looked confused.

"My mom and dad decided to live a lie because they didn't want people gossiping about Ivy having a baby out of wedlock. So we wound up moving thousands of miles away so they could cover up and create this lie. But now Ivy wants Madison to be her baby and not her sister. It doesn't pay to lie. You have to stand up for yourself, Reesa. What do you gain from letting Mamie beat on you like that?"

Mamie gossiped about Pat to anyone who would listen, and had most of the people at church believing her lies. One day, I overheard some of the ladies saying that Pat was a prostitute. That made me furious. Of course, I told Pat about all the lies Mamie was spreading.

As I was getting dressed for church one Sunday morning, the telephone rang. By this time, Mamie allowed me to use the phone.

It was Pat.

"Make sure to save me a seat in church," she said, and hung up.

I was puzzled because I knew Pat hated that church, and said she would never come back to it after she moved out.

When the service began, I kept looking around for Pat from my seat in the front pew. Mamie always insisted I sit there so she could keep an eye on me. I had my Bible and coat on the seat next to me to save it for Pat, but I was beginning to think she wouldn't be coming, since the service was already halfway over.

Just before the minister got up to speak, the doors of the church flew open. As everyone looked around, there was an eerie silence in the church.

I turned to see Pat poised at the double doors. She was wearing a bright red suit with a skirt so short she didn't dare bend over. Her legs looked exceptionally long because of the red high heels, and she had on tons of makeup. Jezebel would have been proud. Holding her head up high and arranging her hat slightly, she took long seductive strides to the front of the church and sat down next to me.

Then, without warning, she kissed me on the lips and, with her fingers, spread the lipstick that she had transferred to my mouth.

"Close your mouth," she said smiling. "It's not ladylike."

The pastor could barely deliver his sermon. Not that it mattered, because I doubt anyone heard a word he said anyway.

After the service, I went home with Joyce and Tommy, and Pat met us there. We all laughed so hard that we were crying. Every time I remembered the look on Mamie's face, I couldn't stop laughing. I carried on like that for hours until my stomach ached.

Pat said, "I simply wanted to teach her a lesson about gossiping."

Mamie never said a word about this incident, nor did Dad or anyone at the church, so Pat succeeded in shutting down the rumors.

About once a week, Dad would slip over to Pat and Walter's apartment and check up on them. Pat had no experience in paying bills, because after Joyce moved out, Dad had me do that. So Pat quickly got in over her head in debt. After that, she handed over her paycheck to Dad every week, and he would pay her bills and give her whatever was left over.

Summer was fast approaching, and Dad had promised that I could visit Aunt Minnie. I was worried about her because she hadn't sounded very good the last few times we had talked on the phone.

But I was excited about seeing Marshall and Melissa again after almost two years.

One day, Joyce picked me up from school, as she often did, and she was beaming.

"What's going on?" I asked.

"How would you like to be an aunt?"

It took me a moment to realize what she was saying. Then I started screaming.

"When?"

"In about six months."

"But you'll be gone to Washington," I said, pouting.

Joyce looked at me and crossed her fingers.

"Maybe we can work something out," she said. "I'm sure I can convince Dad I'll need your help."

With the school year coming to an end, PK and Jackie were looking forward to the big dance and wanted me to go with them. I was sure Mamie would say no, but then the perfect opportunity came up to work on Dad.

That Monday, as he was driving Joseph, PK and me to school, PK blurted out, "Ask your dad now!"

"Ask me what?" Dad questioned.

Poking PK in the ribs, I said, "I just had a question for you. I'll ask you later."

I waited until we dropped off Joseph since I was afraid he may accidentally tell Mamie about the dance. I turned to Dad and said, "Our school is having a Sock Hop this Friday, and I really wanna go. Please, Dad."

PK chimed in, "Please, Mr. Armstrong. We're all going. *Please*, let her go."

"I don't know about a dance," he said. "I've never let any of my kids go to a dance."

"The parents will be chaperoning, Mr. Armstrong," PK said. "Nothing will happen."

"Please, Dad!"

Reluctantly, he finally said, "If I let you go, you have to promise to be on your best behavior."

"Thank you, thank you, thank you!" I said. "But what are you gonna tell *her*?"

I never called Mamie "Mama" when I was out of her presence.

"Let me work that out," he said.

For the rest of that week, I tried to avoid Mamie as much as possible, telling her that I was busy with homework. Since I was usually home on Friday evenings, she would sometimes have me pick up Joseph, and baby-sit him while she went off to a church social. By keeping out of her way and pretending to be doing homework all the time, I was hoping to be free for the dance. My plan must have worked, because when I got home from school on Friday, Mamie and Joseph were gone.

I ran downstairs, because by now I had Joyce and Pat's old bedroom. I quickly changed into a miniskirt that I had kept hidden behind the drawer under Walter's old bed, and ran over to PK's. I was so excited!

PK's older sister, Ivy, took us to the dance, picking up Jackie on the way. Although I didn't have a boyfriend, I had a crush on Ka'Ai, Makai's older brother. I thought he was so cute. But I ignored him because I knew he wasn't interested in me. He always treated me like a younger sister. Nevertheless, I had a ball.

After the dance, a bunch of us walked over to a local burger joint, which was a teen hangout. PK had a guy hanging all over her, and Makai and Jackie did, too. I was the only one there without a boyfriend, but I didn't care. I was so happy just to get out of the house and have fun.

Finally, around midnight, PK called Ivy to come get us.

When she showed up, Ivy told me that Mamie had come to her house looking for me.

"She also sent your little brother over, a couple of times. But I didn't tell them where you were."

I suddenly realized that Dad must have forgotten to tell Mamie about the dance.

Seeing the fear on my face, PK took me by the shoulders and said in a stern voice, "She can't do anything to you that you don't allow her to. No one can step on you if you don't lay down."

I heard her words, but still I was petrified.

As we pulled up to the house, I saw that Dad's car wasn't there. *Maybe I should wait until he gets home.*

"If she hits you," PK said, "you hit her back!"

Apprehensively, I got out of the car and walked up to the door.

It swung open, and Mamie started screaming as soon as I closed the door behind me.

"Where the hell have you been? Do you think you're grown? You're out of control!"

"But Dad said—"

"Go to your room and strip!"

I just stood there without moving.

"I said, go to your room and *strip!*"

"No!"

For a moment, she was shocked. Then she took the extension cord, which was in her hand, and lashed out at me.

I grabbed it and tried to rip it out of her hand, which pulled her forward and almost made her fall.

Gaining her balance, she grabbed my arm and slung me across the room.

My head slammed into a wall, and I fell to the floor. My head was throbbing. Enraged as I felt blood dripping from my nose, I leaped to my feet and ran straight for her, ramming my head into her belly.

She fell backward onto the floor, and I jumped on top of her.

As we wrestled on the floor, I suddenly felt a pair of hands pull me off Mamie. It was Dad.

"Calm down!" he said. "What's going on here?"

Mamie started crawling to her bedroom, yelling at Dad.

"Your daughter's a tramp! She was out after midnight!"

A surge of insanity suddenly hit me. I burst through her door screaming, "If you ever touch me again, I'll *kill* you!"

Dad dragged me out of the room. Overwrought and out of breath, I fell to the floor. In between sobs, I gasped, "I mean it, Dad. I'll *kill* her! If I have to, I'll kill her in her sleep!"

17

Saying Goodbye

After that battle, Mamie and I didn't speak for days. We just avoided each other.

For the first time, I was glad that Joseph was in the house. It was nice to have someone to talk to, especially since Dad was gone so often. I also began to notice that Joseph was becoming more distant from Mamie and closer to me.

On Sunday morning, I got up early to go to church.

When I was ready to leave, Dad and Mamie were sitting at the dining room table, drinking coffee. Knowing that it would irritate her, I walked over to Dad, picked up his coffee cup, and took a sip.

Mamie just glared at me.

"See ya at church," I said as I headed for the door.

"You don't wanna wait?" Dad asked. "We're leaving in five minutes."

"I'd rather walk."

He didn't say anything, because he knew I didn't want to ride in the car with Mamie.

As I turned to go, Joseph came running out of his room.

"Wait for me, Sis," he called. "I'm going with you."

Mamie looked hurt but didn't say anything.

Eventually, Mamie and I had to exchange a few words now and then about household matters, but that was the extent of our communication from that point on. She certainly never laid a finger on me again.

About a week after my big fight with Mamie, Dad came home with bad news.

"I just got a call from Aunt Minnie's cousin Mabel," he said.

"Minnie's had a heart attack, and she's in the hospital. I'm leaving as soon as I can book a flight."

"I'm going with you," I said.

We left that evening on a military plane for California. Two flights later, we arrived the next morning in North Carolina. When we got to Aunt Minnie's hospital room, Dad walked up to her bed and said, "I'm here, Mama."

That really touched me, because I hadn't heard him call her Mama very often.

She was incredibly pale and could only talk in a whisper. There were wires coming from her chest that led to a heart monitor next to the bed. Her breathing was very shallow.

I stood back and let Dad talk to her. I could see in her face how she adored him.

After half an hour, she closed her eyes, and she was gone.

"She hung on to see you two," Mabel said to us.

We went back to our house in Portsmouth to make the burial arrangements. On the morning of the funeral, Mamie arrived with Joseph.

It was a small, quiet service, with perhaps forty people attending—cousins of Aunt Minnie's plus a few friends and neighbors. I kept looking around to see if Marshall and Melissa would show up, but they never did.

After the service, Dad only had a couple of days before he had to report back to duty in Hawaii. However, Mamie wanted to spend some time at the house in Portsmouth. I had no desire to be around her, so I told Dad to leave me at Aunt Minnie's house, and I would close the place up.

Aside from wanting to get away from Mamie, I wanted to see Marshall and Melissa. After Dad dropped me off at Aunt Minnie's house, I didn't even change my clothes before going to find them. No one was home at their grandmother's, so I walked to the corner market to ask the owner, Mr. Thomas, if Melissa and Marshall had arrived yet for the summer.

He looked surprised.

"Miss Pearl and Melissa were in a car accident last summer," he said.

I was stunned.

"Miss Pearl died instantly, and Melissa was in critical condition. Someone told me she also died, but I'm not sure." Seeing the shock on my face, he added, "Maybe I'm wrong. I might be wrong about this."

Slipping out of my high heels, I ran barefoot to Aunt Minnie's house as fast as I could.

All the way, I kept thinking, *It has to be a mistake. He has to be wrong. Somebody would have told me about this.*

I entered the house through the back door into the kitchen and sat down on the floor, totally depressed. The house seemed so quiet and empty without Aunt Minnie in it. Everything seemed unreal, stuck in time. I was too shocked to cry.

Melissa can't be dead. There must be some mistake.

Suddenly, the back door opened. It was Marshall.

I blurted out, "Mr. Thomas said Melissa—" But I couldn't say the words.

Marshall didn't have to say anything. The look on his face said it all.

I just wanted to disappear.

A long shrill came from my abdomen and echoed through the room.

Marshall tried to hold me, but I lashed out, striking him. I crawled into a corner and mourned for Aunt Minnie and Melissa. The pain was so immense that I just lay there for hours, moaning. My exhausted body was soaked with tears and sweat.

Finally, Marshall picked me up and carried me upstairs to the bathroom. He sat me down on a stool and ran some hot water in the tub. Then he helped me to undress down to my slip and left the room.

My eyes stung with tears as I lay back in the hot sudsy water, surrendering to my exhaustion.

After a while, Marshall peeked in, sat down on the floor beside me, and handed me a cup of hot tea. As my trembling hands reached out for the cup, my eyes searched his for answers, but he couldn't look at me. Painfully, with his head down, he told me about the accident. Melissa had just gotten her driver's license and was taking

Miss Pearl shopping. To avoid something in the road, she swerved and lost control of the car, and crashed into a telephone pole. Miss Pearl was killed instantly, and Melissa lasted a week, but her injuries were too severe.

When Marshall finished the story, he pulled a picture from his wallet and showed it to me. It was a little baby girl.

With tears streaming down his face, he said, "She's my daughter. Her name is Melissa. Her mother and I are engaged." He looked at me apologetically. "She was there for me. I didn't want to live. She got me through it. But I never stopped loving—"

I put my hand over his mouth. We just sat there, with him holding my limp hand until the water turned cold.

Finally, he stood up and held out the terry cloth robe that was hanging on the door.

"Let's get you out of there," he whispered softly, turning his head away as I stepped out of the tub.

Slipping on a white cotton gown that I always kept at Aunt Minnie's, I crawled into bed. As I lay there, I heard Marshall taking a shower. When he came out, my eyes were so swollen and were stinging so much that I could barely focus. I tried to look up at him, wanting to tell him that it was alright that he had a baby and was engaged. Instead, I just closed my eyes.

He walked around to the other side of the bed, climbed in under the covers, and curled up against me. I could feel the tears rolling off his face.

There was no sex, no passion, just intimate friendship. We cried until we both fell asleep.

The next morning, when I woke up, I heard Marshall roaming around in the kitchen. I got out of bed and slowly walked downstairs. My body was aching, and my heart felt empty. As I passed a mirror in the hallway, I saw a glimpse of my sad reflection. I looked completely drained.

Marshall had made coffee and motioned for me to sit down.

I dropped into a chair, and he set a cup of coffee and an English muffin in front of me. Then he sat down across from me. He reached for my hand, and our fingers wrapped around each other's.

It was a bittersweet moment. His voice was soothing as he started to speak.

"I'm so sorry, Reesa," he said. "I—"

"I'm not angry," I said. "Our destiny is sealed. I just regret that we shared so much, and I couldn't be there for you or Melissa."

I took his ring from around my neck, but before I could hand it to him, he whispered, "Let it be a reminder that wherever you are, someone loves you very much."

We just sat quietly for a few minutes.

"I'm sorry I didn't come to the funerals," I said. "If I had known, I would have come."

"I'm sorry I missed Aunt Minnie's funeral," he said. "I learned about it too late. I drove all night from New Jersey because I didn't think I could get a flight soon enough. But when I got to the cemetery, everyone was gone."

When we finished our coffee, we talked about what needed to be done to close out the house. We started with the kitchen, taking all the perishables out of the cupboards. We gave all the useful items to neighbors, and everything else we just threw away. Then we went to Aunt Minnie's linen closet and took out sheets to cover all the furniture in the house, which made me very sad because I remembered how much Aunt Minnie had loved her furniture. As Marshall boarded up the windows, it was final. Aunt Minnie would not be coming back.

From the phone in the kitchen, I called Dad. As soon as I heard his voice, I broke into tears. When I was able to talk, I told him about Melissa and her grandmother. He was shocked.

Finally, I said, "I don't want to go back to Mamie's house right now. I can't deal with her. I want to go visit Joyce and the baby."

Dad could tell that I was so upset that I probably *would* kill Mamie if I were forced to be around her.

"Okay," he said, "I'll send you some money."

Marshall insisted on driving me to the airport. When we got there, we held hands all the way to the gate. Then we shared an emotional moment.

As my plane headed for the runway, I could still see him watching from the window of the terminal. I had my face plastered to my own window until he disappeared with a piece of my heart.

As I sat back in my seat, I clung to the phone number he had given me, knowing I would never use it.

I cried during the entire flight to Washington, knowing that I was amputating a huge part of my past.

Joyce met me at the airport with Tommy Jr. He had grown so much, but he was still the most beautiful baby I had ever laid eyes on. Joyce doted on him.

For the next several weeks, I just hung out with my sister and the baby. Sometimes I fell into a deep depression, but seeing my nephew always gave me hope and happiness.

Tommy Sr. and I clashed a little because he still regarded me as a naïve little girl. One time, when I came in late at night, he said, with Joyce standing right there, "You should know better than to come home at this hour. I'm gonna whip ya!"

"No, you're not!" I said. "You might beat me up, but you're not gonna whip me. Because if you hit me, I'm gonna hit you back!"

I've had enough of that with Mamie! I thought.

He laughed, and then Joyce laughed, and then I laughed.

Toward the end of summer, I got a call from Dad in Hawaii.

"Mama's refusing to come back here," he said, referring to Mamie. "You know how she hates it."

"So what does *that* mean?"

"I need you to stay in Virginia with her to help her out."

"What about my friends? What about my school? This isn't fair!"

"I can't help it. She's not gonna come. Anyway, I'll be there in six months when I retire. In the meantime, I'll send your clothes and your school records ahead. And Joseph's, too."

I was really upset. Not only would I have to stay with Mamie, but also I wouldn't get a chance to say goodbye to PK, Makai, and my other friends. I was already missing Hawaii and all the freedom that went with it.

18
Finding Mother

To make me feel better, Joyce took me on a shopping spree, dragging Tommy Jr. with us from store to store. As I picked out clothes, Joyce kept shaking her head, because I bought all kinds of outfits that Mamie would never approve of. But I didn't care anyway.

When we got back to the apartment, we heard the phone ringing as we entered. Joyce ran to the phone with Tommy and picked it up.

After saying hello, she went completely silent. Then, all of a sudden, she sat down on the floor with Tommy in her arms, and started crying.

I took the phone from her, and she left the room.

"Hello, this is Joyce's sister," I said. "Can I help you?"

I was no more prepared than Joyce was.

"Hi, Reesa. This is Mother."

I instantly burst into tears.

Finally, like a broken puppy, I moaned, "Hi, Mommy!"

"Is Joyce alright?" she asked.

We heard a sigh on the line. Then, in a soft voice, Joyce said, "Mother, I'm here."

She had picked up the phone in the bedroom.

At that moment, Tommy Jr. gurgled.

"Is that a baby?" Mother asked.

"You're a grandmother, Mother," Joyce responded. "Tommy's three months old."

"Oh, I can't wait to see him! Send me some pictures."

"How did you get my number, Mother?"

"A private detective got it for me. It's taken me two years to find you all. I petitioned the courts to get custody of you, Reesa,

159

but before the papers could be served, you all disappeared. And the Coast Guard wouldn't tell me where you were."

"Dad moved us to Hawaii, Mom," I said. "I'm only here because Aunt Minnie died."

"Oh, I'm sorry to hear that. She was a good woman."

"How are Chris and Cutie Pie?" I asked. They were my youngest sisters, four and three at the time I left.

"They're fine, honey," Mom replied. "And you have a new brother and a new sister. . . Dalton and Bertha. He's eight and she's seven."

That was a shock to me.

Joyce started laughing. "I guess Tommy Jr. will have playmates."

"I wanna come back to Boston, Mom," I said.

"I'm not in Boston anymore, honey. We've moved to California. A town near San Francisco! I want you to come here with us."

"Great! How soon can I come?"

"I'll make the arrangements from this end. Which airport will you be flying out of?"

"Well, I have to go back to Portsmouth first to pick up my things, which Dad sent ahead. So I guess I'll be flying out of Norfolk. How soon will you have my ticket, because I'll be ready the day after tomorrow."

"I'll take care of it tomorrow."

"Mother," Joyce said. "I'll come out to see you with Tommy and the baby just as soon as Tommy can get leave from the Navy."

We all hated to hang up, but I was overjoyed to think I'd be with Mother in two days.

"Just think!" I said. "When I stopped over in San Francisco on the way from Hawaii, three weeks ago, Mom was right there!"

An hour later, Pat called us. She had just talked with Mother, and was furious with Dad for sneaking us to Hawaii. But now she was planning to move to California, too, as soon as she could save up enough money to get her own apartment.

When Tommy came home, he warned us that Dad still had custody of me, and that Mamie would love to call the authorities on Mother.

"I know," I said. "But I have a plan, and I promise you, she'll let me go."

Mother called back that evening with the flight arrangements, and promised that if Dad didn't let me come, she would come and get me. She seemed stronger than the last time we had seen her.

Saying goodbye to Joyce at the airport the next day was hard, but I was looking forward to seeing Mother.

From Norfolk Airport, I had to take a cab to Portsmouth. It was eleven o'clock in the morning when I arrived at the house, and I had to be ready for my flight to California at nine-thirty that evening.

Mamie wasn't home when I walked in. I went to my old room and quickly packed my clothes. By now it was noon, and Mamie still wasn't there.

I started pacing around the house, worrying that she was spoiling my plans. I felt that I couldn't just leave without talking to her, because she might call the police on Joyce or on Mother.

Finally, I decided to run over to Phyllis's house, but no one was home. Disappointed, I decided to go to my old school to get my transcripts that Dad had sent ahead. I could make it there and back in half an hour.

As I walked onto the campus, I remembered all the times that Phyllis and I had spent here. Meeting her had changed my life, and we would always be friends.

"Hey, what's *your* name?" a male voice said from an open door on the corridor.

"Reesa," I said, trying to make out the face in the dim light.

"Will you be attending school here?"

"No, I'm a transfer student from another state."

"Can I get your number?" he said, stepping out into the corridor.

To my astonishment, it was Alonzo Taylor. For a moment, I looked down, trying to be invisible. Then I suddenly realized that I was no longer a country girl with oversized hand-me-down clothes and no self-esteem. I looked him straight in the eye, and said, "You don't know who I am, do you?"

"No, but I'd like to." His eyes narrowed. "Wait a minute. You're not—?"

"Yes," I said, rolling my eyes. "It's me!"

I walked away feeling empowered. As I left the school with my records, a few minutes later, I knew I would never come back.

When I got back to the house, I knew Mamie was there because I saw her jacket draped over a chair.

I immediately ran outside and crawled under the house. It had been two years, but the coffee can was still there. When I opened it, I found that Walter had left more than a hundred dollars. I laughed and stuffed the money into my pants pocket. However, that's not what I had come for. There was also an envelope in the can. I kissed it and ran into the house.

When I went back inside, Mamie was waiting for me in the living room.

"What's the meaning of *those*?" she said, pointing to my bags, which were sitting by the front door.

"I'm leaving."

"What?!"

"I've spoken to my *mother*. She lives in California now, and she wants me to come live with her. And I'm going."

"I'll have you locked up," she said. "And I'll have *her* locked up, too. She doesn't have custody of you."

"Neither do you."

"We'll see about that! You've lost your little mind!"

At that moment, Joseph came down the hall.

"Just leave Reesa alone!" he cried. "Leave her alone!"

Mamie looked shocked.

I took Joseph by the hand and led him to his room, which was his safe haven. Sitting him down on his bed, I knelt in front of him and said, "I'm sorry I have to leave you, but Dad will be home in no time. I don't want you to get involved in this. It's not fair to you. Just stay in your room. Goodbye, Joseph."

With that, I gave him a big hug.

With tears running down his cheeks, he turned away from me and crawled into a ball on the bed.

I got up sadly and went back out into the hallway. Mamie was in the kitchen, dialing a number on the phone.

"Joseph," she said, "your daughter just came in here, wearing pants and looking like a tramp. She's being disrespectful and says she's going to California to be with Delores. I think Joyce and Tommy put her up to it."

I stormed into the kitchen and screamed right in her face, "Look, who's calling somebody a tramp!"

With an expression of total disgust, she shoved the phone toward me.

"Hi, Dad," I said.

"Reesa, what's going on?"

"I spoke to my mother, and she told me how you hid us from her, and I'm not staying here. I'm gonna live with her, and that's final."

He sighed. Then, sounding very tired and sad, he said, "You and Mamie will have to work this out. There's nothing I can do from here."

"I'll call you when I get to California," I said, and hung up.

I walked into the living room, where Mamie had gone. She was back on the couch, fuming.

I pulled the envelope out of my pocket, took out the contents, and threw them in her lap.

She looked at the pictures of her cuddling with Mr. George, then looked up at me with alarm and disgust.

"There's more where those came from," I bluffed.

Then I calmly walked back into the kitchen and called a cab. When it arrived, Mamie was still sitting on the couch, looking evil.

I took my bags out to the cab and walked back into the house to take one last look. Next to the front door, there were two ugly porcelain lamps that Mamie adored. I knew that they had cost Dad a hundred and fifty dollars each, which he couldn't afford at that time, but she had insisted on having them. With great satisfaction, I knocked them both over with one blow, watched them smash to pieces, and went out the door.

When I got out to the airport, I was a little late and discovered that my plane had taken off without me. I was on standby for the next two flights, but they were filled. Finally, after waiting for hours, I got on a plane that had space for me.

I pushed back my seat and covered my head with the blanket the stewardess gave me. Symbolically, I think I was covering my past—all the abuse, anger, and pain—hiding my secrets.

When I got off the plane in Oakland, California, Mother was waiting for me at the gate. Joyce had called ahead to inform her I would be late. She couldn't believe that Dad had agreed to let me come. I didn't tell her how I had blackmailed Mamie to get away. I didn't want her to think of me as a blackmailer.

In the car, Mother said to me, "Cutie Pie has been so excited about your coming that she got up early this morning, dressed up in her yellow Easter dress, and plunked herself down on a barstool by the front door. She was sitting there when I left for the airport, and I bet she's still there."

Sure enough, when I walked into Mother's house, there was Cutie Pie, waiting for me. I was finally home.

Within a week, I was attending junior college, and Mother was becoming my best friend. I shared everything with her about how Mamie had treated us, and how I had longed to get away.

Pat arrived in California a few months later and got her own apartment, a half hour's drive away.

One day, I told Mother about the recurring levitating dreams I had.

"That's your mind's way of freeing your soul," she said. "That's why the dreams are always so peaceful."

19
We're Family

A few years later, I met my husband, Larry, who was the right fielder for the Oakland A's, and my mother fell in love with him instantly. It took me a while to surrender control, but Mother kept encouraging me to allow my heart to lead. I did and it was one of the best decisions I've ever made. Larry had three children by a prior marriage, so we became an instant family. I vowed to keep all the promises I had made when I was growing up, never to hurt a child. People would meet us and never know I had not given birth to those three kids. I would often tell my children that I had promised to love them before they were even born. They would look puzzled, but would accept what I said.

The first time I got pregnant, I was petrified, remembering Mamie's chant, "If you ever have a baby, every bone in your body will open. And if the bones don't close properly, you'll be crippled for life!" My anxiety and tension led me to have one miscarriage after another.

When I got pregnant for the seventh time, Mother coached me through the entire process. She would call me every day, reminding me I could do this. When Zaae was finally born, Mother held me and we wept tears of joy and success.

It was eight years before I got pregnant again. I remember Mother coming to the house. I was making her coffee and suddenly felt very sick. She got this strange look on her face.

"What are you looking at?" I asked while pouring her a cup of coffee.

"You're pregnant," she said, laughing. "It's *you!*"

"What do you mean, it's me?"

"I had a dream. I didn't know which one of you it was, but it's crystal clear now it's you. And you're gonna have a girl."

She walked over and touched my stomach.

"Look," I said, touching my belly. "I'm as flat as a board. And have you forgotten that I only have one fallopian tube, and the doctors determined years ago it was blocked?"

"Nevertheless," she said, sipping her coffee, "get it checked out. But I'm only your mother and a nurse. What would *I* know?"

Two days later, I found out she was right. I was at the hospital where Mother worked in pediatrics, so I ran up to the fourth floor and showed her the results.

She was so excited that she didn't bother to say, "I told you so."

A week later, before heading up to Reno for the weekend with Pops, Mother stopped by my house.

"Hi, Mom," I said as I let her in. "I thought you were already gone."

She paused in silence for a moment, and then, looking directly into my eyes, she said, "You can do this, Reesa. I have complete faith in you. You're strong, and God created your body for this. Do you understand me?"

I wasn't sure why she had made a special trip over to my house to tell me this, so I just said, "Yes."

The next day, I felt an overwhelming desire to have a picture of Mother, so I went over to her house and let myself in through the back door, which was always unlocked. I went into the family room, where she had a cedar chest in which she kept all the family pictures. I went through every one of them and took the ones I wanted.

As I was heading out the front door, I stopped to look at the two large portraits hanging there—one of Mother and one of Pops. I took Mother's picture off the wall and left.

As I got into my car, I was feeling a little strange.

I must be insane. Mother's gonna kill me when she gets home! She never lets anyone take her photos.

That night, I had the recurring levitating dream. As usual, it was very peaceful.

The ringing of the phone the next morning interrupted my sleep.

It was Mr. Monzo, one of Mother's neighbors.

"This one of Dee's daughters?" he asked with his thick Korean accent.

"Yes, this is Reesa."

"You need to get to your mother's house right away," he said.

"Why?"

"Something happened. Go now!"

And he hung up.

I was wondering which of my younger brothers and sisters had gotten into trouble.

When I arrived at the house, they were all there already. The phone started ringing as I walked in the door. Since I was the nearest to it, I picked it up.

"Are you Delores Alexander's daughter?" an unfamiliar raspy male voice asked.

"Yes."

"Ma'am, this is Officer Friedman of the Hayward Police Department. I'm sorry to inform you that the Reno Police have told us that your mother has passed."

And he hung up.

The room went black. The next thing I knew, I was lying on the floor, and someone was putting water on my face. Friends and neighbors were everywhere.

"Is it true?" I asked.

Someone said, "Your stepfather called and said your mother had a heart attack and died in her sleep."

I pulled myself up off the floor, knowing I had to be strong for my younger brothers and sisters. Someone told me Pat was on the way, but I needed Joyce and Walter around me, too. I reached Joyce right away, but I had to leave a message for Walter.

Mother was the youngest of nine children. I decided to call her oldest brother so he could let everyone else know.

"Hi, Uncle Walter," I said sadly, "this is Reesa."

There was a dead silence on the line. I could tell he immediately knew something was amiss.

"Uncle," I said, choking, "Mother passed last night."

I heard the most horrific groan coming from the receiver. Then it went dead.

During the next hour, all of Mother's six sisters and her brother Dudley called to let us know they were making arrangements to get to us.

Around 3:00 o'clock that afternoon, Pops got back from Reno. Over coffee, he told me that he wanted to divide up Mother's jewelry among her daughters. He kept offering me things like watches, rings, and diamond pendants, but I turned it all down because none of it meant anything to me.

Finally, he said, "You must want *something*."

Without even giving it a thought, I blurted out, "No, I already have what I want. . . " I meant the pictures I had taken the day before.

Then I realized that Mother had let me know she was going to die, and I began to weep. At that moment, it all came back to me. The night before, I had the same recurring dream. This time, it was Mother levitating alone. The higher she went, the lonelier I felt. But she assured me that she was fine. Little did I know that she was implicitly saying goodbye in the midst of a dream.

"Yesterday," I said to Pops, "I came to the house, and I took all the family pictures. I even took Mom's picture off the wall. I'm so sorry. I don't know what I was thinking."

"It's fine," he said. "I'm sure she would have wanted you to have them."

That evening, as I lay in bed, I recalled my last conversation with Mother, and realized that she knew she was dying. Now I could feel her presence more than ever.

It was years before I spoke to Dad again. Often I would call him, but when he answered, I just couldn't speak. I'm sure, though, he always knew it was me.

"Reesa? It's me. . . Daddy."

Holding the phone sobbing, I would simply hang up.

I tried to coach myself to talk to him.

When he answers the phone, just say hello.

But somehow I couldn't.

Of course, sometimes Mamie answered. She just got a quick click.

Finally, I went into my bedroom closet one day, determined to talk to him. I closed the door behind me very quietly, so no one would hear me, and dialed his number.

"Hello?"

"Hi, Daddy."

He started crying.

I cried with him.

Finally, he said to me, "How's your husband and children?" He knew all about them from Joyce.

"Everyone's fine."

"Are you happy?"

"Yes."

Actually, I had recently been pregnant with a little girl we had already named Nicole. But then, in my fifth month, I miscarried and almost died. So I wasn't especially happy.

"I had a dream about you one night, Reesa Baby. You were crying. I kept waking up, but every time I fell asleep, I had the same dream. Are you sure you're okay?"

"Yes, I'm fine."

After that call, I always spoke to him in the closet, or late at night, or when no one was home, always in a whisper, as if I were hiding a dirty secret. I didn't want anyone to question me about him. I didn't want to think about my past or discuss it with anyone. My children seldom asked about my dad, because they grew up with me almost never mentioning him. If they asked about my childhood, I would simply say it was an uncomfortable time in my life and quickly change the subject.

Even with Pat, I tried to avoid dealing with the past. That wasn't easy, because she was very bitter about it, and brought it up all the time. So even though she lived only thirty miles away, I didn't visit her very often. I would call her, though, because it was easier to get out of a conversation on the phone. On those few occasions that I did go to see her, I rarely brought the kids with me, because I didn't want them hearing about our past.

One afternoon, the phone rang, and Larry answered.

"It's your dad," he said, looking alarmed as he handed me the phone.

"Hi, Daddy," I whispered as I headed toward the bedroom.

I heard labored breathing on the other end of the receiver.

"Hey, Reesa Baby...Daddy's in trouble." He moaned as if he were in pain.

Trying to sound calm, I choked back my tears and said, "I'm coming, Daddy."

20

Healing from the Inside Out

"Ladies and gentlemen," the stewardess announced, "we're approaching our final destination, Norfolk Airport. Please fasten your seatbelts."

I sat up, realizing that I was finally being forced to face my past head-on. For twenty years, I had been trying to block it out. I even kept Joyce, Pat, and Walter at a distance, because they reminded me of that painful past. Now I was about to come face to face with Mamie for the first time since I had knocked over the lamps and walked out the door, twenty years before. I would not be able to hang up on her or ignore her. Dad had been trying to make peace between her and me for a while now.

"Do you wanna talk to Mama?" he would ask.

"She's not my mother," I would say, "and don't call her that."

"She raised you."

"No, she *trained* me. Besides, the phone works both ways. She owes *me* an apology."

I wasn't expecting any apologies now, but I certainly intended to tell her how I felt.

How hateful and mean you were, I would say. *And how unnecessary that was! What a waste of energy! It takes so much more effort to be mean than to be nice. You must really hate yourself to carry that much bitterness inside. The only good thing that came out of your being so cruel is that it taught me exactly how NOT to behave. I've raised five children, and I've never mistreated them, not even once.*

As I climbed down the steps from the plane to the tarmac and walked slowly toward the terminal, I didn't recognize anything because the whole airport had been completely remodeled in the twenty years I had been gone. A clock near the gate said it was a little after 9:00 p.m.

My plan was to get my bags and catch a cab to Dad's house. But when I got to the baggage claim area, I heard a voice call out, "Reesa!"

Looking around, I didn't recognize anyone.

I must be hearing things.

"Reesa!" the voice said again.

I turned and saw an elderly couple standing about ten feet away. The man was balancing himself on a walker, and the lady holding on to him was hunched over.

"Daddy?"

It was more a question than a statement.

Tears rolled down his cheeks as he held out his hands to me.

I ran to him and embraced him to keep him balanced. With my head on his shoulder, I looked at the old woman beside him.

"Hi," I said softly.

"Hi," she said with a quiet, broken voice that was barely recognizable.

I took Dad's hands and placed them on his walker.

"How did you get here?" I asked, looking around for a driver.

Surely you didn't drive out to the airport in this condition.

"We took a cab," Mamie said. "Your daddy didn't want you at the airport all alone."

I sighed with relief that Dad hadn't tried to drive.

Grabbing my bags from the carousel, I said, "Let's get a cab."

That's when I noticed that Mamie couldn't walk without holding on to Dad's shoulder, and could only go five or ten feet at a time before having to rest.

This is not going to work. At this rate, it'll take us three weeks to get outside.

"You sit here," I said to Mamie, helping her to a chair, "and I'll come back for you."

Dad and I went outside and hailed a cab. Dad lowered himself into the car, and as the driver put his walker and my bags in the trunk, I headed back to Mamie and brought her out on my arm.

As she held on to me for support, I realized that this was the first time in my life that she and I had physical contact without me being abused.

During the twenty-minute ride to the house, no one said a word. I was too shocked by their obvious physical deterioration to know what to say.

When we got to the house, it was clear we were all going to go straight to bed. Mamie, who could get around the house better than she did at the airport, put Dad's pajamas out on the bed.

He sat down on the bed and started crying.

"I fixed up your old bedroom for you," Mamie said.

I went over to Dad and kissed him on the cheek. He was still crying softly.

"Goodnight, Dad."

I turned to Mamie and choked out a "Goodnight."

I didn't know what to call her. I couldn't possibly call her Mama. Not after all those years of being forced to call her that.

As I closed the door behind me, I heard her say to Dad, "She still hates me."

I walked into my bedroom and dropped my bags. Looking around, I saw that everything was just as I had left it twenty years before. The bed and the dresser were where they had always been, the same curtains covered the window, and the same bedspread covered the bed. For the first time, I realized that the bedspread was baby blue. When I had grown up in this house, everything had seemed so monochrome.

As I brushed my teeth in the bathroom, old memories drifted by. There was Joyce secretly calling Spence. There was Pat in her scalding bath. There was Walter swatting me in the nose to get blood for my faked period. And there was Joseph, being adored by Mamie.

Standing at the door of my room, overwhelmed by these old memories, I passively allowed the tears to roll down my cheeks.

I wanted Mamie to be strong the way she was when I was young.

I wanted to tell her how much I hated her.

I wanted to stand in her face and say, "I'm not that scared eleven-year-old little girl you used to beat with an extension cord."

I wanted to scream, "I don't have to call you Mama...because you're not my mother."

I wanted to wrinkle the blankets on my bed, mess up my clothes in my drawers, and leave the closet door open.

I wanted to make Mamie a plate of beans and force her to eat them at the table in the cold garage, where we had so many meals.

I wanted to burn that extension cord that she *still* had hanging on her bedroom doorknob.

I suddenly realized that the past had held me hostage for all these years. Shame, loathing, and revenge had controlled me. Bitterness was my companion, for I had breathed in the toxin of hatred for over twenty years, and it had polluted my system. Mamie had won!

During all these years, I had not told a single person about my past, except my mother. Larry didn't even know, and none of my children knew. And because of that, I had robbed my children of their grandfather and their aunts and uncles. I had always known that we all start to die from the moment we're born, but now I realized how anger and hatred speed up that process, like a virus slowly growing inside and destroying the spirit and the soul. I crawled into my bed, and in that moment of silence, with my heart empty, paralyzed by emotions, I succumbed. I no longer had the will to hate. Suddenly, all the artificial barriers that I had constructed to protect myself came tumbling down. Realizing that *I*, not Mamie, was accountable for all the suffering I had caused my family and myself for the last twenty years, I cried myself to sleep.

The next morning, I called home and talked to Larry and my kids, telling them I would be bringing their grandfather home. Before I could get dressed, Dad was standing at my door.

"I made you breakfast," he said. "Come and eat."

As I followed him down the hall, I noticed that he was walking better than he had the day before, and wasn't depending so much on the walker.

As we entered the kitchen, Mamie was sitting at the table, drinking coffee. I didn't know what to say to her, so I didn't say anything. There was an awkward silence in the room for a moment as I looked down at the sausages, eggs, and pancakes that Dad had prepared.

Then, looking up at him, I said, "Where's Joseph? Does he come by and check on you guys?"

Looking embarrassed, Dad said, "Joseph's too far away. He's got a family to raise. Besides, he doesn't drive...he doesn't even own a car."

"That's no excuse," I said, looking at Mamie.

Her face tightened.

Just at that moment, the doorbell rang.

As I headed toward the front door, a short, plump nurse about my own age let herself in. Putting down her medical bags, she walked up to me and gave me a big hug.

"You must be Reesa," she said. "I'm Sylvia. Mr. Armstrong told me his baby was coming to see about him. He talks about you all the time. You live in California, don't you?" Before I could answer, she looked around and asked, "Did any of your kids come with you? He wanted to see them so bad."

"Yes, I'm Reesa," I said. "And, no, none of my kids came with me."

By this time, we were entering the kitchen. Sylvia went straight up to Dad and took his plate away from him.

"Mr. Armstrong!" she scolded. "You *know* you can't eat these things!"

He put his head down like a naughty boy.

"Have you even checked your sugar level today?"

He just looked away.

"Of course, you didn't." Turning to me, she said, "Your dad's a diabetic and has high blood pressure. He's supposed to be on a special diet, but it's difficult to make him stick to it. Twice within the last month, I've found him here in a coma. If I hadn't arrived when I did, the situation would be much grimmer. Either someone's gonna have to live with him, or he'll have to be admitted to a veterans care facility."

"There's no one here who could live with him," I said sadly. "Everyone lives out of state."

Dad was looking so sad. I began to wonder if he thought I was coming home to stay. The mood in the room was so bleak. But when I realized that they thought I was simply going to stay a while and go back home, I blurted out, "They're going back to California with me."

Dad smiled, but he had tears in his eyes.

"Mama," he said, "I told you Reesa was gonna take care of everything."

He started to stand up, as if he were going to his room to pack his bags.

"Sit down, Mr. Armstrong," Sylvia said playfully. "You're not leaving this minute. Besides, I have to show your daughter how to check your blood sugar."

She opened one of her bags and took out a kit. I walked over to watch.

"Reesa, are you familiar with any of this?"

"Yes," I said, "my mother was a diabetic... and also a nurse. She taught us all how to do injections."

Sylvia looked a little confused for a second, knowing that Mamie was neither a diabetic nor a nurse. Then she handed me the kit.

"Alright, let's see what you know. I'll walk you through it."

I thought about the first time I ever gave Mother an injection. I was about seventeen at the time, and had to attend a couple of classes at her hospital to learn how to give the shots. She also taught me how to check her sugar level and what to look for if she had taken too little or too much insulin.

"Okay, you *do* know what you're doing," Sylvia said after watching me check Dad's blood sugar level and give him a shot of insulin. "I come every morning at the same time, but no weekends. That's when Mr. Armstrong gets himself in trouble." She gave him a playful nudge. "So, how soon are you leaving? I can help you out if you need me, and you can call the church. Some of the deacons will be glad to assist you."

"*I'll* call the church," Dad said, pouting. "Those are *my* friends. I'm not helpless."

Rubbing his shoulders, Sylvia said, "Alright, you call the church, and we'll get everything else in motion."

I looked over at Mamie, still not knowing what to call her.

"How about you?" I asked. "Do you want to see your sister before you leave?"

She timidly shook her head yes.

I kept looking for the old Mamie to surface, to give me an excuse to lash out at her. But that Mamie no longer existed, so I couldn't retrieve an ounce of anger.

For the next three weeks, I called home every day. Poor Larry was trying to hold everything together until I could get home, but the kids were excited about meeting their grandfather. Larry went out and bought a queen-size bed and a dresser for the guestroom, and my oldest daughter, Shalonda, prepared the room.

It took me three weeks because I had to get all of Dad's and Mamie's records transferred to California, go through all of their belongings to decide what would stay and what would go, and to sell or give away most of the furniture. Just before leaving, I covered all the remaining furniture with sheets, promising Dad that I would make more final arrangements when I got a chance to come back.

After storing the car in the garage, I did my final walkthrough. The deacons from Dad's church helped out during this time, and boarded up the house after we left.

On the plane, Dad was like a little kid, all excited to be meeting his grandchildren. Larry had purchased first-class tickets because he felt that it would be easier on Dad and Mamie. When we landed at San Francisco International Airport around seven that evening, Larry was at the gate, and I ran straight into his arms. As we hugged, I realized how much space he gave me. After all, I was bringing Dad and Mamie to live with us after twenty years of never talking about them, and he totally accepted them.

I grabbed his hand and pulled him over to Dad and Mamie.

"Larry," I said, a little awkwardly, "this is my dad...and his wife...my...uh, stepmother."

I had said it and was still alive.

Larry hugged them both.

"Let's get your bags," he said. "The kids are excited to see you all."

As our car pulled into the driveway, I could see faces peering out the window. Suddenly, the front door swung open, and one by one the kids rushed out to greet us. Amid all the hugs and laughter, Larry and Zaae, my fourteen-year-old son, began unloading the bags from the trunk.

When we settled into the house, I said, "Children, this is your grandfather... and his wife."

As they came up to hug Dad and Mamie, Dad gave each one a nickname, and they all loved it.

Mamie sat down in a corner and kept to herself. Shalonda noticed this and tried to include her in the party, but she remained withdrawn.

After everyone retired for the evening, I went to check on Dad. The guestroom door was slightly open, so I could hear Mamie crying.

"I know I did wrong by them," she whimpered, "but I didn't know how to love them without getting hurt myself."

"Well, you better figure it out, Mama," Dad scolded, "because we're here to stay. And I'm not giving up my grandchildren for no one, and that's final." Then he lowered his voice a bit. "Mama, didn't I tell you this was gonna come back to you someday? All you had to do was love them. They were just kids."

"I know," she said sadly. "But I was scared after seeing my aunt adopt those two kids. You've seen what they did to her after they found their real mother. They left her alone to die in that big old house by herself. Then they came back, sold all her property, and ran off without looking back."

"But you were selfish, Mama. You was always selfish."

I was stunned... first of all, because Daddy was finally getting a backbone and speaking up for us. And second, because Mamie was actually trying to justify her years of abusing us. Overhearing this conversation, I literally lost my balance and almost fell through the door as I knocked and walked in at the same time. Walking over to Dad's side of the bed, I tucked him in and leaned over to kiss him on his forehead.

Mamie shut her eyes, as if to shield herself. I slowly walked to her side of the bed, tucked her in, and asked, "Are you comfortable? Can I get you some tea?"

She shook her head no. I could see tears in her eyes. Bending over, I kissed her on the cheek. I felt more powerful than ever, knowing that hatred for her would no longer control my life. At that moment, I just felt totally sorry for her.

As I gently closed the door behind me, I heard Dad say, "See, Mama? I told you she doesn't hate you."

She started crying softly.

Walking away from that bedroom, I realized that Mamie had always been operating on fear. The fear of being rejected had fueled her need to control everyone and everything, and this had been magnified by her illiteracy, which kept her ignorant. Fear and ignorance had caused her to inflict so much pain on us. But those were *her* demons. I would no longer allow them to control me.

I immediately picked up the phone and called all my siblings, announcing that we were going to have a family get-together. Joyce agreed to fly in from Colorado, Walter agreed to fly in from D.C., and Pat was already in town. We all decided to meet in two weeks.

Later that evening, I phoned Joyce again.

"Hi, J," I said. "I owe you an apology and an explanation."

I called her "J" now because that was Tommy's nickname for her.

"An apology for what?"

"I've been hiding from the past all these years. Being around you, Pat, and Walter has always reminded me of the torturous years, so I've been avoiding you guys."

She started crying. In the past twenty years, she had always called me. I had never called her. And I had only seen her twice in all that time, when she came to visit me.

"Reesa," she said, "I've always known you were hiding."

"I'm sorry for the time our children have missed together, and the wisdom, courage, and loving that can only come from family."

All this time, I was sitting in bed next to Larry, who was listening intently to everything I said.

When I got off the phone, I said to Larry, "I'm sorry. I'm sorry that I've hidden everything from you throughout this time."

Without saying a word, he put his arm around me. Relieved that I had finally been able to reveal my story to him without his judging me, I fell asleep in his arms.

Around two o'clock in the morning, I was suddenly awakened

by the sound of music. I got up and crept downstairs. Dad was in the family room with the kids. He didn't even have his walker. There was rap music playing, and everyone, including Dad, was dancing.

When the music got a little too loud, Dad put his forefinger to his lips.

"Shhh! Don't wake your parents," he whispered.

I sat in the dark on the stairs watching him carrying on with the kids. They obviously all adored him.

Suddenly, he saw me and went limping for his walker.

As I headed down the stairs, he announced, "I was just trying to get something to drink."

"Sure you were," I said, rolling my eyes at the kids. "Now, go to bed, all of you. Shame on you for having your grandfather carry on like that."

"Okay, mom," Zaae said, dancing over to click off the stereo. "But Grandpa is dope. You should see him dance."

As I went back to bed, I realized that Dad wasn't quite as dependent on his walker as he had let on, probably to get some sympathy from me, hoping I would bring him to California.

Wind Beneath My Wings

In the next two weeks, I had a lot of work to do because all our families would be together for the first time ever. I had to call everyone, make arrangements for their lodging, and shop for food for seventy mouths.

Joyce and her family were the first to arrive, a day before the gathering. And Walter arrived the next day. Pat and her family, plus aunts, uncles, and cousins trickled in from as far away as Ohio.

That afternoon, at the park, Larry barbequed ribs, chicken, and links; using his special sauce that he took so much pride in. In addition, some relatives brought salads, baked beans, and many other side dishes.

We played baseball by family teams, and of course my family won, since Larry had played right field for the Yankees and the A's, and all of our children had some athletic skill. But they wouldn't let me play, because they knew I was no good. So I got to be scorekeeper.

After the ballgame, some of us played charades, with the women playing against the men.

At some point, maybe an hour into the party, Mother's sister, Aunt Emma, showed up. She was always late and always arrived on the scene with a different hair color. We had actually set up a door prize to whoever guessed what color she would show up with this time. It was bright red, and Walter got the prize.

I chuckled as I saw my mother's brother, Uncle Dudley, go behind a tree with his soda can. Everybody knew that he poured out the soda and refilled it with his favorite spirit.

My younger brothers and sisters, who knew nothing of my past with Mamie, were happy that all of Mother's children were together at last. It was something my mother had promised them years ago.

My stepdad, Pops, was passing out change to all the little kids, who were waiting for the ice cream truck.

I walked up the side of a hill so I could get a picture of everyone. Afterward, I just sat there watching them. An outsider would think it was a picture perfect family. Mom's sister, Aunt Emma, as always, was cheating at a game of spades at one table. At another, Uncle Walter was arguing with someone over a domino game. Several of the little ones were playing hide-and-seek, and some of the adolescent girls had a game of double Dutch going. Standing around grills and tables, people were eating, drinking, and laughing.

Walter came moseying up the hill and sat down beside me. He didn't need to say anything. I lay my head on his shoulder. It had been a long time since I had felt like his little sister. He was still my rock.

Soon, Joyce and Pat joined us. We all just sat there in silence, watching our family playing and dancing.

Dad had some little ones on his lap and standing around him. From his motions, we could tell that he was reciting his famous story about a little boy who only had a head.

"There was a little boy who only had a head," he would say. "He used to sit at the window and watch the other kids play. 'I wish I had a body,' he always said. 'I wish I had a body.' Then one day he woke up and had a body! He ran across the street to play with the other kids, and was hit by a car and instantly killed. The moral of the story: Quit while you're a head!"

Joyce, Pat, Walter, and I laughed when we saw Dad pantomiming that story.

Then I looked off to the side and saw Mamie. She was sitting all alone, fumbling with her cane. No one went up to her. Not even the children. She was a pathetic invalid, just waiting to die. There was no point in being angry with her anymore. That hateful Mamie no longer existed. Time had turned her into a broken old lady.

Suddenly, there was a commotion down below. The teenagers had been challenging each other to a dance-off, with Dad and Uncle Walter as the judges. Now the two old men were challenging each other to a dance-off.

Everyone looked up at us on the hill and started waving for us to come down. Hand in hand, we ran down the hill, with the wind at our back, the past behind us, pushing toward the future, gliding like birds without wings.

Reina Murray has been a successful business owner of VIZIONS INC., for twenty years. She attended Laney College where she studied Business Administration. Though *Birds without Wings* is Murray's first book, she is also a successful playwright, having written and produced plays such as *Windows of Time* and *The Miracle of Christmas*. When she is not managing her hair salon business or writing, she is coordinating weddings and co-producing her up-coming film, *Cover Up*, a short film addressing the AIDS epidemic. Murray now resides in Hayward, California, with her husband, Larry Murray, youngest daughter, and grandchildren Madison and Xavier.

Sylvester I. Okoro was born and raised in Nigeria. Mr. Okoro received an MBA degree from Holy Names University, Oakland, California in June 2007. He earned his Bachelor of Science degree in Business Administration from the then California State University, Hayward (now California State University, East Bay, Hayward Campus) in 2001. In addition, Mr. Okoro received a diploma in International Business and Marketing from the University of California, Berkeley Extension in 1997 and a diploma in Journalism from the Nigerian Institute of Journalism, Lagos in 1992. Mr. Okoro is also a successful published writer. His articles have appeared in many publications including the California State University Hayward's *Pioneer Newspaper*, *The Daily Californian*, *The Berkeley Daily Planet*, and the *Daily Times* of Nigeria. Mr. Okoro was the founder and pioneer president of African Student Association at California State University, Hayward. Mr. Okoro is the founder of RespectAfrica.Org, a non-profit educational outfit that provides unbiased reports and news about the African continent. Presently, Mr. Okoro is a bank manager at the US Bank, and resides in Hayward, California.

REALITY BECAME THEIR DEMISE AND THE THOUGHT OF DEATH BECAME THEIR FREEDOM. THEY WERE IMPRISONED BY THEIR STEPMOTHER'S DEMONS, TORTURED OUT OF FEAR, AND HELD HOSTAGE FOR YEARS.

Based on a true story, *Birds Without Wings* chronicles the memory of eleven-year-old Reesa as she and her three siblings—Joyce the voice of reasoning; Pat, the rebel; and Walter, the protector—are propelled into a world of abuse. Their father's love puts them in harms way. Their stepmother's ignorance and silent frustration imprisons them. Their mother's vulnerabilities bruise their souls and scar their hearts. The ransom for their souls has a price tag that no one can quantify. Their cries are echoes that cannot be heard. They are four helpless birds looking through the windows of their souls, awaiting their way of escape to freedom.

"Reina Murray's *Birds Without Wings* is an autobiography of hope and triumph. A riveting narrative of child abuse, love between siblings, and ultimate and inevitable victory. Reina finds closure through forgiveness and acceptance of her circumstances and a compassionate understanding of her abuser's helplessness and fears. The novel is a celebration of spirit. It is a story of love, healing, and sympathy. A must read for anyone working in the areas of child abuse, foster care, or generally interested in the welfare of children."

Vibha Puri Chandra, Ph.D.
Dept. of Human Development and Program for Women's Studies
California State University, East Bay, Hayward Campus

"This is a powerful story of how a young girl endured years of abuse from a malicious stepmother and learned to survive and eventually flourish in her adult life: a touching testimony to the resilience and courage of the human spirit."

William A. Sadler, Ph.D.
Author of The Third Age: Six Principles of Growth and Renewal After 40
Professor of Sociology and Business
Holy Names University, Oakland, CA

Spiritual Growth, Christian Living

978-1-6024700-1-9

51499

9 781602 470019

US $14.99 | CAN $19.99

TATE PUBLISHING
& Enterprises